Additional Praise for

It's Not Where You Start, It's Where You Finish!

For many years I have known the power of stories, the importance of motivation, and the purpose of surrounding myself with people who impact others with a punch. YOU WILL LOVE Gillian's ability to move you in the direction of your own personal dreams. I have personally watched her live these principles. Mary Kay Inc. has provided many of us the platform to tell our story. Many people have stories to tell but this one is sure to make a difference.

Gloria Mayfield Banks
Harvard University, MBA 1982
Independent Executive National Sales Director, Mary Kay Inc.

Gillian Ortega is a unique lady who has overcome numerous obstacles since leaving Ireland at 18 years of age with $20 in her pocket! She was on her way to America to pursue the "American Dream" . . . and she has certainly achieved what she set out to do!

As an Independent National Sales Director for Mary Kay Inc., she has climbed to the top! Along her journey, she has inspired, motivated, and encouraged thousands of women to believe they too can turn their dreams and goals into realities! You will love this book, and it will produce incredible results in your life!

Rena Tarbet
Independent Senior National Sales Director

Every so often a book stands out as clearly exceptional . . . so well written that your soul urges you to keep turning the pages. *It's Not Where You Start, It's Where You Finish* is one of those books! With a refreshing style all her own, Gillian Ortega uses her down-to-earth wit and wisdom to ignite your belief in what's possible, raise your level of expectation for your future, recognize your potential and empower you to take a step ahead of the crowd into a lifetime of success. A must-read for anyone committed to living their dreams!

Lisa Diane
Author, *When You Can Walk on Water Why Take the Boat?*

I often find that those who have lived outside the United States have a much deeper appreciation of the word "freedom" and "opportunity." Such is the case with Gillian Ortega. Her awe and wonder of this land, she experienced over 20 years ago, still feels fresh as you turn each page. *Its Not Where You*

Start, It's Where You Finish will help you see your world through different eyes. Gillian lives the American Dream.

Linda Toupin
Independent National Sales Director Mary Kay Inc.
Creator of 'Choices' CD

In pursuit of her American Dream, immigrating from Ireland, Gillian's success story impacted my heart and my dream of being a Major League player in the United States. She inspired me to reach for the levels of excellence I had dreamt of. Her basic philosophy of "God Blesses Excellence" will impact your very soul. This book will encourage you at all levels of your life to reach for your highest accomplishments. Her favorite saying is "the doors of opportunity are marked PUSH!" You won't be able to put this book down. INSPIRING

Albert Pujols
St. Louis Cardinals
National League Rookie of the Year 2001

Everyone wants to finish well, but few get out of the starting blocks mentally equipped for the complete journey. In her book, *It's Not Where You Start, It's Where You Finish,* Gillian Ortega shares the nuggets of truth that ensure both starting and finishing with results and excellence. Gillian's common sense, other's-focused philosophy is one you can implement and make your own on the road to living your wildest dreams! From someone who uniquely knows what it means to "Live the American Dream" with success, Gillian has made herself a master student of life and business. Now as Master teacher, she is passing it on to you!

Pamela Waldrop Shaw
Author *Design Your Life 90 Day Planner*
Independent National Sales Director, MKI

Gillian is one of the most motivational leaders I have met. She inspires people to reach farther and stretch beyond the comfort zone and into greatness.

Her personal story is one of inspiration and struggle, but she perseveres and becomes one of the top leaders in the Mary Kay organization.

Don't make the mistake, "Oh, she's just one of those pink cadillac ladies and has nothing to do with my business." Gillian Ortega has practical, straight-forward ideas and tools to help any organization or individual move to the next level of success.

I would recommend Gillian Ortega's book to anyone who desires success in their life.

Guy F. Hulen
Director of Human Resources
Hong Kong Shanghai Banc Corp.

It's Not Where You Start, It's Where You Finish!

The Success Secrets of a Top Member of the MARY KAY Independent Sales Force

Gillian Hennessy-Ortega

WILEY

JOHN WILEY & SONS, INC.

Published by John Wiley & Sons, Inc., Hoboken, New Jersey.
Published simultaneously in Canada.

For general information on our other products and services please contact our Customer Care Department within the United States at (800) 762-2974, outside the United States at (317) 572-3993 or fax (317) 572-4002.

Wiley also publishes its books in a variety of electronic formats. Some content that appears in print may not be available in electronic books. For more information about Wiley products, visit our web site at www.wiley.com.

Library of Congress Cataloging-in-Publication Data:

Hennessy-Ortega, Gillian.
It's not where you start, it's where you finish! : the success secrets of a top member of the Mary Kay independent sales force / Gillian Hennessy-Ortega.
p. cm.
ISBN-13 978-0-471-70974-9 (cloth)
ISBN 0-471-70974-3 (cloth)
1. Selling. 2. Selling—Vocational guidance. 3. Success in business. 4. Hennessy-Ortega, Gillian. 5. Mary Kay Cosmetics. I. Title.
HF5438.25.H463 2005
658.85—dc22

2005000714

Printed in the United States of America.
10 9 8 7 6 5 4 3 2 1

This book is dedicated

to my mother,
whose life taught me to never give up;

to our heroic men and women in the military
who daily put their lives on the line to keep
America free; and to

Mary Kay Ash, who founded a company
dedicated to "Enriching Women's Lives."

Here at our sea washed sunset gates shall stand,
A Mighty Woman with a torch whose flame is the
  imprisoned lightening
And her name "Mother of Exiles."

Inscribed at the Statue of Liberty
Written by Emma Lazarus (1849–1887)

Contents

Foreword

The large meeting hall in the Kansas City Convention Center was packed as the woman leaned over to take a leather jacket from a man. As she put the jacket around her, you could see that it was not just a leather jacket, it was a leather jacket that was made in the image of an American flag.

American troops had just gone into Iraq and as the audience saw the jacket the chatter subsided and all eyes were on the wearer of the jacket as she began to speak. She told of her humble beginnings in Ireland and of the struggles in her past. She told of coming to America with little more than the $20 bill in her pocket. Then she told the moving story of how that Irish girl of humble beginnings had overcome adversity and accomplished exceptional success in her new home, "the land of the free."

It was an awe-inspiring speech, but the evening was not over. She asked anyone in the audience who had husbands, sons, or relatives serving in the military to stand up. One by one, hundreds stood up as an indication that they had family serving in the military. As time seemed to stand still for a brief moment, a song began to play on the center's loud speakers. It was Lee Greenwood's "Proud to Be An American." Less than three minutes later, there was not a dry eye in the house. Her own compelling story combined with her fervor for the country that gave her the chance to live it was a passionate testament to the power within all of us to overcome our obstacles and live a full life.

That was my introduction to Gillian Hennessy-Ortega, and the extraordinary rags-to-riches story of a little Irish girl who came to cherish her new home, America, so much. What happened in that auditorium is simply "Gillian." After writing *More Than a Pink Cadillac,* I was invited to travel to various parts of North America and talk about the book. As I traveled across the United States and Canada and visited with many of the one million Independent Beauty Consultants that work with her, I heard a lot of "Gillian" stories. That is why, when given the chance to read the original manuscript of her book, I not only wanted to read the entire manuscript, but I wanted others to read it as well.

As I read the book, I found a lot of compelling and empowering ideas for anyone who wants to better their lives or change their future. If there is one thing that I have found in common among truly successful people, it is that most have had to overcome tremendous odds in order to succeed. You will find a lot of stories about such people in this book.

One of the important things that Gillian does in this book is to point out that personal success is not about having some formula or reaching one specific goal. She makes a great case for committing to a life of self-discipline, personal excellence, and ethical behavior. I believe she is correct: Success has much less to do with process than it does with the character of the individual.

Gillian begins the book with a summary of her own life and the obstacles she faced as a young girl in Ireland. In subsequent chapters, she writes about the basic personal and character issues that underlie personal success. She illustrates each idea with the story of someone she knows in the independent salesforce of Mary Kay Inc. who emulates that quality. She also explains in almost every chapter how the Mary Kay priorities of "God first, Family second, and Work third," Are instrumental to the success of these individuals. I trust that you will find that this is a book that will inspire you to seek excellence in your own life.

If you are at a time in your life when you need inspiration or direction, I recommend this book. The same is true if you've simply given up, if you feel that you are stuck in a deadend career, or unable to advance. This is a book about overcoming the odds and becoming someone exceptional. It's not just a book that is applicable to those in the selling field. I believe these principles will help you regardless of where you choose to claim your future. I hope you enjoy it as much as I did.

Jim Underwood
Author of *More Than a Pink Cadillac*

Preface

One of the most surprising things I have discovered about the sales profession is that sales and life are quite similar. In life, you get out what you have put in. In sales, your success depends on your effort. I think that describes my purpose in writing this book. My sales career has changed my life.

I am an Independent National Sales Director at Mary Kay. There are about 300 of us in the world. Each one of us got there the same way: We earned it. It was hard work, it took a lot of commitment, but it was worth it. If you are not familiar with the Mary Kay organization, I would like to tell you a few things about it and my relationship with the company.

Mary Kay Inc. was founded over 40 years ago as a cosmetics company. The founder, Mary Kay Ash, was a woman who had excelled in the sales profession, but had often been held back because she was a woman. She founded Mary Kay because she wanted women to be able to "have it all." To Mary Kay, "having it all" meant that a woman could live a life in which "God first, family second, and work third" was the premise. Based on that premise and the golden rule, Mary Kay Inc. has become a world wide organization with over one million independent beauty consultants world wide.

I also need to explain a few other things about Mary Kay Inc. You may not know that a significant percentage of the cost of most cosmetics is advertising and marketing. Mary Kay believed that it made a lot more sense to work through people and pay those monies to those who sell the product. That approach is called *direct marketing*.

You will note that I am an "Independent" National Sales Director. That means I own my own business, I don't work for Mary Kay Inc. I am an independent contractor. That means I have the freedom to work as much or as little as I choose. It also means that I have the ability to put the important things in my life ahead of my business.

In this book, I will talk a lot about people who earn the use of a career car (a mid-sized car) or a pink Cadillac. Those are some of the achievement awards that I can earn as an Independent Consultant. They are based on my performance and the performance of the people that I bring in as Independent Beauty Consultants.

I felt it was important for you to understand those details before you read the book. Now, I would like to talk about the book and why I wrote it. You will note that the book is laid out in three parts. The first part, Chapter 1, is about my life, how I came to America from Ireland, and how I began selling Mary Kay products.

The second part is about three keys to personal success: respect, reach, and rejoice. I believe these are the foundation to successful lives. The third part was developed for my speaking. I needed a way to clearly explain the basics of sales success. The "10 principles of sales success" are based on not only own sales career, but the success of others. These are the things that I like to talk about when I am speaking to sales professionals, whether they are new or experienced.

You will discover that this is not a sales "method" book. At the same time, I truly believe that if you apply the 10 principles you will be a successful salesperson. I believe that sales success and life are a lot alike. I also believe that you have the opportunity to control your own happiness, just as you are the only person who can make you a successful sales professional.

It is my hope that this book will help you understand just how much of your own happiness you hold in your hands. Success is simply a by-product of establishing your life goals and making the commitment to go for them. That's my hope for you. You already have the ability to achieve your dreams, now all you have to do is to make the commitment.

Gillian Hennessy-Ortega

Acknowledgments

I want to acknowledge my Mom and her role in influencing and encouraging me throughout my life. Your passion for life through all of your trials inspired me my entire life. I love you, Mom.

This book is the result of a lot of team work. I want to thank Matt Holt of John Wiley & Sons for taking my original idea and helping me create a book out of it. Of course, I could not have completed the book without the constant coaching of Shannon Vargo of John Wiley & Sons.

My encourager, and the calming voice in my life throughout this project has been my agent John Willig of Literary Services Inc. This book would not exist had it not been for John.

I appreciate the hard work and gentle spirit of Melinda Hanson-Perry of Mary Kay Inc. She has been a joy to work with and has been extremely helpful to me throughout the editing of this book. Special thanks to Tracy Geise and the entire creative works staff for getting the book through the review process. I appreciate Greg Franklin's help during the "final push" to get the book finished.

This book and my career would not have been possible without all of the encouragement, teaching, and coaching that I have received from numerous Sales Directors and National Sales Directors. You touch the lives of people every day. You have taken me to a new level of excellence on my journey to my American Dream!

I so appreciate the love and support I received from my husband and son through the process of writing the book. I started writing this in December of 1999 and throughout the process you both were my biggest cheerleaders. You know how much I love you.

I want to thank my sisters for their support, and especially my sister Donna in Ireland, who told me many years ago to share my dream with others in the USA to help them step into their greatness. Love you, sis.

To my extended family, the Ortega's: You have loved me from the first time we met and are a constant source of strength for me. You know how much I love you all.

To my Aunt Annette and Uncle Val who financed my first trip to the USA. Without you both, I would never have been able to travel to the United States at age sixteen to capture my American Dream. I will be forever grateful.

I want to thank Angie Oniawa for sowing the seed in my heart for pursuing the book. I love you, my friend.

Finally, I must salute the founder of Mary Kay Inc., Mary Kay Ash. She has been my inspiration. I am just one of the many she has blessed around the world. I thank God for you.

PART I

From Ireland to America

Chapter 1

Taking Charge of My Life

In some ways, I was at the end of a journey. In others, it was just a beginning. As the jet turned to land at JFK International airport in New York, I looked out the window and caught a glimpse of the Statue of Liberty. There she was, standing majestically as if watching over this great land.

I had long dreamed of coming to America to discover my destiny. Although my return ticket was dated almost exactly one year from today, I knew in my heart that this was to be more than just a year. It was going to be the beginning of my new life and my future. As scared and alone as I felt, I also had feelings of exhilaration and anticipation. I was coming to America to discover my American dream.

The day I arrived in America, I was eighteen years old, had only $20 in my pocket, and a dream in my heart. I had accepted a position as a nanny and I was to be paid the generous sum of $20 per week, plus the use of the family car. While that might not seem like much to most people, to me it was a lot. I had grown up in Cork City, Ireland, under emotionally and financially challenging circumstances, so this opportunity seemed like the chance of a lifetime.

Grand Beginnings

When I came into the world, I was born into what some might call an Irish fairy tale. My mother had been swept off her feet by her suitor, William L. Hennessy, and they had been married with celebration and joy. My mother had coal black hair, green eyes, and an enchanting personality to match her beauty. My father was a handsome, vivacious man who came from an impressive Irish family. It seemed to be a match made in heaven.

Their wedding was one of regal splendor. They were married at the local Catholic Church. The townspeople lined the streets after the ceremony to applaud the new bride and groom as they rode in their Bentley to their reception. Yes, it was almost like a fairy tale.

My mother and father had some wonderful times in those early years. Although my father sometimes drank too much, they seemed to be getting along well and his business was successful. Shortly after they were married, they discovered that my mother was expecting her first child. They were both delighted to be starting their family. During childbirth, my mother experienced complications and had a stroke. The baby was healthy and strong, but the doctors advised that my mother would never be able to live a normal life again. As a result of the stroke, she would be partially paralyzed for life.

My father adored his daughter, but could not deny that he had always hoped he would one day have a son. Although her doctors were emphatic that my mother have no more children, my mother and father decided that they would try to have another in hopes of having a son.

When my mother became pregnant, the doctors refused to care for her since she had disregarded their advice. My parents traveled to England so that she could have specialized medical care. Their second child, my sister Jackie, was born, and both mother and baby got through the delivery without incident. The birth of Jackie was soon followed by the birth of three more girls, Me, Toni, and Donna. William, the only boy was born after Toni. At last, my father had his son.

By the time I was born, my father's drinking had become a serious problem. He began drinking more frequently, becoming more outwardly aggressive toward his family, and going out more often. Mae Barry, the nanny my father had hired when I was born, provided much of the needed stability and encouragement that my mother as well as her children needed. She was often the only stabilizing force in the household.

By the time my brother was born, my father's drinking had become extremely detrimental to the family. He began to be abusive to my mother. But being Irish Catholic, divorce was not an option for my mother and father.

As I grew older, I dreaded the nights when my father would come home in drunken rages. It seemed that each episode became more and more extreme. But Mae was always there to encourage us and to take care of my mother. Through it all, Mae was there to give our lives stability and love. In many ways, she was our "silent defender." She always made sure that we were cared for and that we knew that we were loved. Mae had a powerful impact on my mother as well. My mother, in spite of her disability, was a very strong woman.

Throughout my life, Mae had been there to be my mentor and my encourager. She was there for me from the time I was born. She influenced my life in a powerful way. When I was 8 years old, Mae became very ill. She was diagnosed with cancer. Her condition quickly deteriorated to the point that she was no longer able to care for us, and she was hospitalized.

Not long after, my mother took me to the hospital to visit Mae. As I walked into the room, I saw Mae, a mere shell of what she had been only a few weeks earlier. Mae asked my mother if she could talk to me alone. After my mother left the room, Mae took my hand in hers and said: "Gillian, you must take care of your mother for me and be my eyes for her when I cannot be there." I promised Mae that I would care for my mother. Mae died a few weeks later. I was devastated. My mother's helper and our mentor was gone.

Later in my life, I realized what Mae had given me. During my childhood, she had always encouraged me to "reach for the stars." She said I was never to finish second; she always wanted me to do my best.

Peace in Adversity

To this day, I do not understand how my mother was able to endure not only the unbelievable tragedy of having a major stroke as a young woman, but further having to live with the abuse and alcoholism of my father. Through it all, she held her head high as if there was no pain or humiliation. It was my mother who taught me my first lesson about persevering in life. My own life experience and my mother's words taught me that there are two choices in life: You can be a victim or you can be a victor. I am fortunate that my mother taught me how to be a victor even during life's most difficult times.

I have never forgotten what my mother told me on the day I started the first grade: "You've got to be number one." That was the way my mother was. Even though she was disabled, she inspired her children to be exceptional in everything that they did.

After many years of abuse by my father, my mother could take it no longer and filed a criminal complaint against my father. My father was furious and moved out of the house. Although he continued to support the family financially, we saw little of him during those years.

When I was 12 years old, my father contracted pneumonia. A few days after we learned he was ill, my mother came in to my room and sadly told me: "Gillian, your father passed on to be with God."

A Nightmare Begins

The funeral was a trying time for my mother and our family. After attending the graveside service, we all returned to our house where I overheard some relatives talking about what a pity it was about my father's business. After everyone left, my uncle stayed to talk with my mother. My father had changed his will and left my mother out of it. But there was more. My father's business was insolvent. In addition to all of her other difficulties, my mother had to take care of liquidating my father's business. It felt like we were still living with my father's alcoholism and its consequences.

My mother was left with only the house that she and my father had been given at their marriage. She was disabled and left alone to care for six children, her only income a widow's pension of $85 a week. We also discovered that a number of our friends no longer wanted to associate with us. In the eyes of the community, we had been disgraced. I often overheard children at school talking about how my father had left us penniless.

Never Give Up

During this time, our lives radically changed. Living on a widow's pension with a family of seven is just about as close to poverty as you can get. Despite our circumstances, my mother was never discouraged. When we could not pay to heat the house, she bought a coal stove for the living room and we would spend cold winter evenings in front of the stove playing games and having fun.

My mom also became an exceptionally creative cook (although we ate bread, potatoes, and beans a lot, she prepared them in many different ways so we hardly ever realized the monotony of dinnertime). At times, my mother would tease us and make all the sacrifices and all her hard work seem effortless. In spite of all the losses in our lives, we were blessed as a family. My mother was a champion. In spite of our limited resources, Mother also saved a few pennies along the way so that occasionally we could go into town and buy some candy or ice cream.

During this time, my teacher, Mrs. Nolan, became a tremendous influence in my life. The events of my childhood had left me feeling discouraged and hopeless, but Mrs. Nolan took an interest in me and became my encourager. She convinced me to become involved in musicals and school plays. That led to an opportunity to join the Monfort Singers and Dancers. While I was a performer with the group, they were invited to go to America to perform. Although my mother did not have the money to send me, she asked my uncle Val if he could help buy my ticket. He agreed! I was going to go to America.

My trip seemed like a dream. The group was divided and stayed with volunteer host families while we performed, and we got to tour America. It was an inspirational time in my life. This was the first time I saw the Statue of Liberty. Little did I realize at the time that the trip was an overture to my future.

The Call

One wintry evening after I had returned home to Ireland, our telephone rang. One of the host families from my visit abroad had recommended me to an American couple. They wanted to know if I would consider coming to America for a year to work as a nanny for their three-year-old daughter.

I had just turned 18, so for most girls it would have been a time to leave home. But I had promised Mae that I would care for my mother. One evening I heard my mother slowly making her way up the stairs to my room. "Gillian," she said, "I think the opportunity to go to America is one that you must accept." I knew it broke my mother's heart, but it was clear that she thought it was best for me.

Time became a blur as Herb and Charlotte Watchinski, my new employers, came to Ireland with their daughter to pick me up. I immediately fell in love with little Karin. My sister Mary gave me her new dress so I would have something to wear. The evening before my departure, my mother came into my room and tearfully said goodbye. She pressed a 20-pound bill into my hand. I knew that was a lot of money to my Mom. I tried to return it, but she insisted I take it.

America, the Beautiful

When I arrived in America, I was homesick, frightened, and excited all at the same time. My new home was to be in Kansas City, Missouri. I arrived and got settled in, and things began to go fairly well. Each day, Karin would cry when her parents left for work. I decided that my job was to make her as happy as possible. I spent my days taking Karin to different places and keeping her happy and entertained while her parents were away.

One day Karin and I were alone at home and I was trying to figure out how to operate the drain in a sink. The plumbing in Ireland is quite different from that in the United States. I had reached a point of total frustration, when the doorbell rang. It was our neighbor, Jackie. I was so relieved that I had someone to help me figure out how to operate that drain. Of course, it only took Jackie about a second to explain how to operate it.

Jackie and I struck up an immediate friendship. She told me that her husband was a police officer and suggested that we go and meet one of his single friends during their dinner break one day at a local restaurant. I agreed, but I was a bit anxious. I had not really dated much before.

The day for our dinner came, and Jackie and I drove up to the restaurant where we were to meet Jackie's husband and his friend. It turned out that the friend had been dispatched on a call, so the dinner would probably be off. At that moment, another squad car pulled up and as the window rolled down, I saw the most handsome man I had ever seen in my life. Under my breath I said, "My goodness, it's Ponch!" Growing up in Ireland, I had watched the show Chips and Erik Estrada (Ponch) was one of my favorites. I would dream of finding a man like him to spend the rest of my life with. There I was, 18 years old, and the moment I saw him I told myself he was the man I would marry.

Vince Ortega spent his dinner hour talking with me. He was the most respectful man I had ever met. We began dating a few months later. Since I had to care for Karin, Vince decided it was best to make Karin a part of our dates. They became so fond of each other that even on my days off, Vince would plan dates that Karin could be a part of.

A few months after we started dating, Vince asked me to meet his parents, John and Anita. I was anxious about meeting them, but once in their home, I discovered a loving family, just like mine. Vince has five brothers and sisters just like I do. I adored Vince's mother the moment I met her. Vince's father, John, and I also immediately developed a close relationship. John is a man of deep convictions and integrity. In many ways, John has become the father I never had.

At the end of my year in America, one afternoon Vince asked if we could call my mother. He asked her if she would give her consent for me to marry him. Vince suggested that he buy an airline ticket for my mother to come to America to visit us. She agreed.

The day came that my mother was to arrive and I was anxious to say the least. We met her at the airport and immediately went to Vince's parents' house for dinner. There was really no need for me to be anxious; my mother and Vince's parents immediately liked each other. Most importantly, my mother loved Vince. When she met him, she called him "her Godsend."

A Journey Complete

A year later, Vince and I were married. I finished my fourth semester in college and landed a job in the technology department of a local company. We had a son, Vince Jr., who became the other light in my life. After Vince was born, I wanted to spend more time being a mom and less time working or commuting. While discussing this with a friend in the ladies' room at a restaurant, a woman interrupted us, saying, "I have the solution." I was offended at first to have a stranger listen to my conversation, but I decided to hear her out.

The woman was a Mary Kay Independent Beauty Consultant. I was interested, but we did not have the extra money to invest at the time. I asked Vince his opinion and he was wary of the situation. One day the woman called and asked if she could stop by. I told her to come after Vince left for work. Once I heard the details of the opportunity, it did not take long for me to decide what to do. I had hidden one of Vince's credit cards for the occasion, and I placed my first order that day.

That evening when Vince got home around 11:00 P.M., I was nervous. I cooked him a wonderful dinner and told him I had something to tell him. I explained what I had done and, much to my surprise, when he saw my excitement, Vince encouraged me to go for it. What I didn't know was that Vince (now a police detective) had done a background investigation on Mary Kay Inc. He ran the company through the Federal Bureau of Investigation, Internal Revenue Service, and Better Business Bureau records and finally he talked to his financial advisor who told him, "Mary Kay is the most progressive company in America today and your wife would be crazy if she at least didn't try it." I didn't have much choice but to be successful. I wanted to be sure I could pay off Vince's credit card before the payment was due.

I set myself a goal of working my business for six months while still working a 60-hour work week. After a month, I was earning the same take-home pay in nine hours selling Mary Kay products as I was working 40 to 60 hours for someone else. Exactly six months after making the commitment, I left my full-time position and began selling Mary Kay products full time.

During a short visit to Ireland, I told my sister Donna about what I was doing. Donna looked at me and said, "How many people have you told about this wonderful opportunity?" Up to that point I was content selling the products and I had not thought about recruiting others to sell it, even though I understood that is how you advance in your business. That was a turning point for me. I made the decision to begin working my business like I should have been all along. I returned to Kansas City with a new dream in my heart.

My business took off like a rocket. I began earning incentives like the use of a career car and vacations. The most satisfying moment was when I took my mother to Hawaii. I had earned the trip for Vince and myself as a reward for my sales production, but had been doing well enough financially to buy Mom a ticket to go with us. We rented a condo right on the beach for my mother. One day I walked into my mother's room and found her out on the balcony room painting. She told me she didn't want to forget all the beautiful things she was seeing. Although she had never painted in her life, it had been one of her life-long dreams.

As I walked out on the patio, there my mother stood, with tears in her eyes. In front of her was a breathtaking painting of the Hawaiian coastline. She looked at me and said, "Gillian, thanks to you and Mary Kay I have had the opportunity to live an unbelievable dream. God knew what He was doing so many years ago when the doctors didn't want me to have any more children, yet I went against their counsel. Where would I have been without you in my life?"

At that moment, I felt that God had led me to America so that I could achieve my American dream and achieve dreams for my mother. Today, I operate my own business that generates income not only for me, but also for all the people that have counseled me. My mother no longer has to depend on her widow's pension for her livelihood. She has her own bank account that my sisters and I contribute to. We call those her fun accounts. She now spends four to six months each year with Vince and me.

As an Independent National Sales Director, I am often asked to travel and speak to women around the world. I am one of the most blessed people around. I have the opportunity to live my American dream—and to share that dream with others.

Sell Your Way to the Top!

This book is about selling, but more than that, it is about life. I have been blessed in my sales career. I have my own business, I work when I want to work, and I am one of those fortunate people who has time for her family.

I believe that God wants the very best for you. If sales is your chosen career, I hope you will discover that mediocre is not an acceptable goal. I hope you realize that when you are "average" you are as close to the top as you are to the bottom. So, why not go for the top? It is my dream that you strive for the exceptional. It is not all about money—it's all about life!

PART II

The Three Keys to Personal Excellence

Chapter 2

Respect

A desire for personal excellence is the foundation of personal performance. Personal excellence is a goal we must strive for at each step we take in our lives. It is both reflected in and influenced by the attitude we take toward each decision or objective we face. If we choose to perform according to a standard of excellence, the result will be success. Unless a person possesses certain attributes, it is doubtful that they will ever achieve their life goals. At the heart of personal excellence is respect. Respect involves seeing the value in yourself as well as in others. Having respect for yourself and treating others with respect is essential to any relationship, and vital to your ability to succeed.

As a person who makes her living selling products, I tend to closely observe sales personnel when I shop in stores. In some cases, I learn a lot about how to better relate to my customers. In others, it is little more than a lesson in how to fail.

We often do not associate the idea of respect with that of sales. However, the presence of one is essential to the success of the other.

Being able to develop a relationship is the first step in being successful in sales. I want to stop for a moment and provide a little insight into the vital role respect plays in sales. Here is an example of what many women might remember about their last car purchase experience.

I Want to Buy a Car!

When I became a National Sales Director, I was thrilled with the prospect of receiving cash compensation to purchase the car of my choice. By then I had recruited enough people that I was now running my own small business and was an Independent Sales Director. My dream since childhood was to own a Mercedes Benz like my aunt and uncle drove in Ireland.

I set out to visit the car dealer in our town that specialized in that particular brand. My dear friend Angie, along with my husband joined me in the endeavor. We walked into the showroom and out of the corner of my eye I noticed a salesman looking us up and down. He didn't come over to help; he just let us roam the showroom floor.

I saw the car of my dreams. I was excited . . . and tried to catch the eye of the salesman. Finally, he meandered over to us with much hesitation. The impression I got from him was that we were not welcome on his showroom floor.

I asked him if we could test drive the CLK 430 and his reply was abrupt and disrespectful, "Well, I don't think that car is suited to you. Why don't you look at this model here that is less than half the price?" For a moment, I was taken aback at his response. That was not the treatment I expected from a salesman wanting to sell a car. I looked at him and said, "I beg your pardon, that is not the car I want to purchase. I want to purchase the CLK." He replied, "Well, you can't test drive this model; you will have to go to the used car showroom to see if you like it."

I was appalled at his lack of respect for the fact that I as a woman wanted to purchase a car of that class. As I walked out of there, I was confronted with the emotions of inadequacy I felt as a young girl in Ireland when I didn't have the money to even imagine owning a car like that. But it was a different time I reminded myself as I made my way over to the used car dealership with my friend and my husband, all of us stunned at the treatment I had just encountered. We walked into the used car showroom and explained to the dealer what had happened. He was extremely apologetic and said that was not how they operated their dealership but they have had some problems with that salesman and his incredibly disrespectful attitude.

The gentleman took us for a ride in the used model CLK and I fell in love with it right away, saying, "This is the car for me." When we got back to the used car dealer's office, I made sure that he talked to the management to let them know what had happened. The used car dealer began his sales pitch on the used model, saying that they could give me delivery right away and would make me a deal of a lifetime.

Now I felt that I was in a situation similar to the one with the previous salesman. I had just shared with this man what I did not care for and he attempted to turn the story to his advantage to convince me to purchase the used car instead.

I sat there in amazement and said, "Sir, you do not understand, I want to purchase a new car. I worked hard to earn this privilege and NEW is what I will have."

He finally gave in and said, "I am not supposed to sell new cars here but I will ask the management." After another lengthy wait while they apparently debated the issue, they agreed to allow him to sell me a new car.

He wrote out my order and we left. Upon leaving, my husband and I felt battered and belittled by this experience. We had started out on our expedition to buy a car in high spirits, feeling proud to be able to walk into a dealership and make this purchase. We left feeling that this was the last place that we wanted to spend our money.

Because of this treatment, I decided to wait a week or so before agreeing to purchase it from this dealership. We searched the Internet to see if we could have the same car delivered from another dealership. The downside was that my car would have to be serviced at the dealership from which I purchased the car.

In the meantime, the used car salesman called every day and when I told him we were contemplating what to do he said, "Lady, you either want the car or you don't, so which is it?" Unbelievably rude, all he wanted was a quick sale for his own gratification. I knew then that I could not give my business to that dealership.

My husband had a great friend in the car industry and talked to him about the experience. He knew the manager of the dealership involved and made a personal call to him for us. The manager was incredibly apologetic and asked if he could call me. He said, "I will sell you the car myself without commissions to get your business and your trust back." We went in to meet him, really liked him, and ordered the car.

The day my car arrived, my husband and I went to pick up the car. Talk about poetic justice. The salesman who was so degrading to us just six weeks earlier was there as we walked in to the showroom floor yet again. His manager had dressed him down about the incident and he now knew he lost the sale and the commission because of the way he treated us as customers. He lost out on a long-term relationship and an immediate sale.

Treating Others with Respect

Women in America today have the income and the right to purchase any car they desire. He attempted to deny that right by his actions. That was a huge error in judgment on his part. It is all about respect.

That story is played out every day at car dealerships around the United States. Often, in addition to the almost insulting way we are treated as women buyers, we find ourselves faced with another common issue in the car business. "Just a minute," says the salesman. "Let me ask my manager to come out and talk with you. This price is so low, that only a manager can approve this sale."

Now let's be honest about what is really going on. The "manager" is nothing more than another salesman. He has been watching you behind a one-way mirror that overlooks the sales floor. (The salesmen take turns playing "manager" for each other.) The salesman introduces you to the "manager" and explains the transaction in front of you. Inevitably, the "manager" says, "Are you ready to drive this car home today if I approve this deal?"

That's Not Respect!

If I had told this story in front of a group of women, they would all be nodding their heads in agreement. Each one would have a number of similar stories. Most people can immediately pick up on the fact that you do not respect them. Respect is something that is conveyed nonverbally. People readily recognize whether you do or do not respect them. Women will often listen more to the nonverbal signals you send them than the words you use. And trust me: We know when you do not respect us.

Mary Kay Ash, the founder of Mary Kay Inc. always made sure that the first thing new Beauty Consultants heard was the golden rule. She took "do unto others as you would have them do unto you" and modified it a bit. She simply said "seek the best for others." She also said "Imagine everyone you meet has an invisible sign around their neck that says 'Make me feel important.'" Mary Kay believed that sales success would be a given if you would first focus on finding what is best for others.

Mary Kay spent much of her time helping others. Her joy in life was watching others succeed. She was someone who would pass up a sale if it was not the right thing for the customer. She was unwavering in "seeking the best for others." That is why so many of those who knew her continue to tell stories today about how she impacted their lives.

Developing Respect for Yourself

Sometimes, we have to discover just how great God made us in order to be able to instill that in others. If you were to meet Nelli Kirkpatrick today for the first time, you would see a wonderful, dynamic, and very successful person. If you had known Nelli before she started her Mary

Kay career and then met her again today, you might not believe your eyes.

Nelli began her Mary Kay business in 1986. Nelli told me of how she started "with no formal education and a skin problem." In the past, she sought the help of dermatologists, but that did not seem to help the problem. Nelli did not wear make-up due to her skin problem.

Nelli had been invited to try Mary Kay products on a number of occasions, but had never felt that it was something for her. In 1986, she decided she would quit her job so she could stay home with her young children. After a while, she became a little bored, but really had no idea of what she wanted to do. She had no interest in sacrificing the time she now had with her three children.

Finally, on a whim, she accepted an invitation to go to a Mary Kay meeting and have a facial. A friend that she had gone through high school with had called and asked her to go to the meeting. "Can you imagine," said Nelli. "I was immediately sold on the benefits of the product."

"One of the things about the company that immediately got my attention was the commitment to God first, family second, and work third." Nelli, a committed Christian, said that she felt right at home when she attended her first meeting. That first meeting had such an impact on Nelli, that she made the decision to become an Independent Beauty Consultant that night. She was especially impressed with the fact that she could be there for her children and husband when she needed to be, but could have a business as well.

Nelli had a few hurdles to overcome in her new career. "I was terrified of speaking in front of other people," said Nelli. "I had no self-esteem and really did not respect my own ability to contribute value to others." Nelli goes on to tell of some of the experiences she had in those early months. She recalls that day by day her confidence in herself and her abilities began to increase. "One thing that really helped me," said Nelli, "were the other women in my adopted sales unit. They have so much respect for others, especially my adopted Sales Director . . . they don't care where you've been; they just want to help you understand your own capabilities. That is what this company is all about: Everyone is about instilling self-confidence and inspiring others." One of the things that Nelli realized is that most if not all of the consultants who were encouraging her, had previously had similar feelings about themselves. "I finally decided that if they could do it . . . I could, too!" said Nelli.

At the end of her first nine months, Nelli received a major sales award. But even after her early success in sales, she was reluctant to take the first major step in what is called the Mary Kay career path, and accept the position of Independent Sales Director. Nelli had no interest in being a sales director because that meant that you had to speak in front of more than five people at a time. Finally, Nelli gave in to all of those who were encouraging her and began her progress up the ladder of success. Today, Nelli has reached the position of Independent Future Executive Senior Sales Director. Along the way,

Nelli has done what everyone else did for her. She spends her time working with other people just like her. Now she has her own successful, but growing business. Interestingly, Nelli's theme for the new national area she is developing is "We can make a difference." Truly, Nelli is a person who is making a difference in the lives of others.

Nelli has had a phenomenal experience. She became an Independent Sales Director in 1989. She's gone on to earn the use of 12 career cars over the years, including three pink Cadillacs. I think what is most impressive about Nelli is the respect she has for herself and others. When she began her quest for success, Nelli had no respect for her own abilities or talent. She had no self-respect. That is why I say that respect begins with self-respect and ends with respecting the value of others. Nelli did not think she was capable of achieving what she has done when she first began her Mary Kay business. Nelli does not have a National Sales Director who is responsible for mentoring her, so I adopted her through the adoptee program to become a member of our area. By her own admission, Nelli did not begin her business as someone who had overwhelming self-confidence. I know that has changed, and along the way she has become one of the most accomplished and respected people I know. I got a note from Nelli that describes what happened:

> In my wildest dreams I could not have imagined the great things this business could provide me and my family. The Mary Kay opportunity has helped me build my faith, self-esteem, confidence, and has given me the most incredible friendships. Mary Kay has awarded me with fabulous

prizes like furniture, over seven carats of diamonds, the use of 12 career cars, and many more treasured gifts. Dreams really do come true in this company.

I find it inspiring when I see someone who has been through the same experiences that I have. Like me, Nelli had to deal with feelings of inadequacy as she started selling. Nelli, like most of the successful Independent Beauty Consultants that I have met, did not begin as a "natural salesperson." What she and many others have are a lot of people just like them surrounding them and encouraging them to make the commitment to become exceptional.

After all, who wants to live a mediocre life when you can be exceptional?

It's All about Respect

I met a man recently who told me about a car-buying experience that he had. I think it demonstrates just how important respect can be. He told of how he was looking for a new car. The first dealership he pulled in to was loaded with new cars, and lots of salespeople. At first, he thought that the president of the United States might be there, because all of the salespeople were wearing trench coats and had two-way radios in their hands.

The first salesperson was really aggressive, and immediately started on the worn-out sales pitch, "If you find the deal you're looking for, are you ready to buy today?"

It didn't take long for my friend to leave and go to another dealer. At this dealer, the salesperson was at least polite and listened to him. That's when he went into the psychological "bait-and-switch" pitch of "let me introduce you to my boss." Of course, the "boss" (who was really another salesman) asked, "If you find the deal you're looking for, are you ready to buy today?" My friend was immediately turned off.

Then he went to another dealership, even though he expected to get the same type of treatment. This time, however, the salesperson was polite and really seemed to care about finding out what my friend really needed. There was no "required" process to go through, the salesperson just listened to him and tried to figure out exactly what he needed. My friend, a knowledgeable salesperson himself, asked the salesperson how long he had been in sales. The man told him he had been in sales for one month. He then asked him how he liked working at the dealership. The man began talking about how it was a lot like a large family. He also mentioned that he especially liked the way he was trained to deal with customers. "We don't have a sales pitch, our owners just want us to help people find what they need. They believe everything else will take care of itself if we just help people."

Respect: That's the difference between how my friend was treated at the various dealerships. Nelli discovered her personal potential and went from nowhere to the top because she was treated with respect. The people around her treated Nelli with such respect that she realized she had a great deal of value. Over time, as she was continually surrounded by people who clearly communicated their respect and appreciation for her as a person,

Nelli discovered just how capable she really was. There was a champion hidden inside Nelli, and her new found friends helped her discover it.

The Golden Rule of Sales Success

Earlier I talked about the Golden Rule. It applies to selling just as much as it does to any other part of life. Seeking the best for others is not something you can fake. It has to become a part of your being. Treating others like you would like to be treated is a standard that is difficult to achieve.

In the same way that I came from Ireland so many years ago with a new dream in my heart . . . having a desire to help others, that is the key to your sales success. Can you imagine? We all like to have friends, but think about how many friends you will have if you become a person who starts looking out for other people? When it comes to selling, you will have a lot of customers who simply will not consider doing business with anyone else but you.

A Personal Example

A few years ago, I met a young woman named Laurie Bierbrodt. In the direct-selling business, one of the ways you can build your own income is by recruiting new people into your unit. I have found that when I apply the "seek the best for others" principle in my own life, I am doubly blessed. Laurie moved to Kansas City after starting her business in another city. One of the Mary Kay traditions is that a Sales Director can adopt consultants whether it will be financially beneficial or not. It's the "Mary Kay way." Laurie was one of those people. When I met Laurie, I immediately knew that we were going to be great friends.

Laurie has been a Mary Kay Beauty Consultant for 11 years. She started selling Mary Kay when she lived in Memphis, Tennessee. She left her full-time corporate position so she could stay home as a full-time mom. Laurie later had another child. Laurie and her husband agreed that when the youngest child entered the first year of school, that she would either be a Sales Director or she would go back to work in her corporate job again.

As the time approached for Laurie's youngest child to enter school full time, her husband reminded her of their agreement. Up to that time, Laurie had focused on doing just enough business for incidentals and not much more. It was a fun way for Laurie to earn a little extra money without giving up time with her children. When her husband reminded her of their agreement, Laurie decided to dedicate herself to becoming a Sales Director. I like to call that "making the commitment." Four months later, Laurie earned her first career car and one month later she qualified for Sales Director. For the uninitiated, a career car is an achievement award at Mary Kay. It means that you get the use of a car (you pay the insurance, gas, and oil) for two years.

In June of 2002, Laurie attended my debut as a National Sales Director. At that time, she decided that she needed to focus on making National Sales Director by 2007.

Six months later, Laurie's husband unexpectedly died of a heart attack. Laurie has such tremendous inner strength. She got through her tough times, thanks to her faith in God and the support of her friends from Mary Kay. In the two years since her husband passed away, Laurie has committed to achieving financial independence with her Mary Kay business. In the first year after her husband's death, Laurie had her best year ever. She may be able to double that amount this year. I got this note from Laurie that tells just how much all of her Mary Kay friends have meant to her:

> My National Sales Director, Maria Aceto, and my Senior Sales Director, Sherry Dutcher, and all of my Mary Kay family of friends offered so much support that I was able to make it through the most difficult time in my life. My faith in God is the reason that I am still able to get through each day. My purpose in life now is to mentor other women, and to teach them that they can be more than they think they can be. That you don't always know what tomorrow will bring. Life is a journey, and you should always look at each day as a gift and enrich other people's lives and that in turn will enrich your own life.

Laurie is one of those people who is a daily inspiration to me. Just like so many others, Laurie is on track to achieve phenomenal success. Laurie is someone who lives the principle of respect. She showers those around her with appreciation for who they are and encourages them to become what they can be.

Respect, Success, and Humility

You become a person of respect when you decide that you want to make a difference in the lives of others. We have all met our share of people who are on ego trips, but when someone comes along who truly respects you, they make a difference in your life. I am thankful for all of those people, like Nelli and Laurie, who have come into my life to make it a little bit brighter. I am also thankful for those who believed in me long before I was able to believe in myself. I thank God daily for how He has allowed me to live this American dream.

Chapter 3

Rejoice

I want to begin this chapter by asking you to think back and identify some of the most rewarding and fulfilling moments you have experienced in your life. What events in your life immediately come to mind as "crowning moments"? Most people will tell you that the most rewarding times in their lives occurred when someone else publicly recognized them.

You may remember the saying coined during the 1992 presidential campaign to state the obvious: "It's the economy, stupid." When it comes to success the obvious truth is that "It's not about the money." I've also heard it said that money is not success, but simply the way a sales professional keeps score. My observation of salespeople tells me that they are motivated more by that moment of recognition, when their managers and peers surround them to "rejoice" than by the money.

A few years ago after a former football player lost a major lawsuit, the court told him to sell everything he had. One of the things he refused to sell was his Super Bowl championship ring. A symbol of recognition for a success few achieve, the value of the ring to the player wearing it is immeasurable.

Rejoice and Revitalize

In my role as an Independent National Sales Director, I have had the privilege of observing many Consultants receive awards given in recognition of superior performance. I often notice that there are others in the crowd who are equally if not more excited than the person receiving the award. Frequently, family members and Sales Directors are most proud of the Consultant's achievement. I have a mountain-top experience when one of the Consultants achieves something wonderful. I become revitalized and get excited about my work all over again.

I have seen people from almost every profession leave their careers to pursue a Mary Kay business. There are teachers, accountants, and even some corporate-level officers of companies among the ranks of the Mary Kay independent sales force. Now let me paint a picture for you: People leave jobs with guaranteed incomes to become Independent Beauty Consultants where they are starting at zero. There is no one to guarantee them anything and they are just like any people who decide to go into business for themselves. Why in the world would anyone want to do that?

I believe people want to rejoice. Rejoicing is a way to revitalize ourselves and our goals. Most of the people that begin a Mary Kay career believe that there is more available for them as an Independent Beauty Consultant than there is at a company sitting behind a desk for eight hours a day. At most companies, there is no rejoicing. People are not revitalized by simply showing up for work, doing their job, getting a paycheck, and leaving at 5:00 P.M.

Many people that I talk with are completely discouraged with their jobs. They may make a lot of money, but the bottom line is that they are demoralized instead of revitalized in their careers. There is an entire company that creates products that focus on this problem. At www.despair.com, you will find an entire company that has been built around the notion that despair is a common occurrence in the corporate experience. I was recently looking at their web site and found that they have announced a new online magazine (*BooHoo!*) that is expressly for the discouraged and downtrodden. Obviously, it is a satirical and comical approach to dealing with work life, but there is a lot of truth contained in the things they discuss.

A New World

I was like a lot of others who were not pleased with their work life. Like many of the other Independent Beauty Consultants at Mary Kay, I wanted the opportunity to call my own shots, to work my own schedule, to be with my family, and still enjoy my work. I simply did not want to work for a company; I wanted my own company. If I were to summarize the reason that most people give for starting their own Mary Kay business, I think that's it. But there is more.

Being in business for yourself can be a lonely and challenging situation. In fact, most people will tell you that after about six months of being in business for yourself, you may be ready for despair.com. With a Mary Kay business, things are different. The Mary Kay Independent salesforce includes nearly 1.3 million people worldwide and all of them are committed to helping each other. Sure, there are a lot of women who just want to make a little extra money. But there are a lot of women who want to have their own business that provides them with an opportunity to earn an income and be their own boss. In the case of those people, they consider helping others to be successful is one of their responsibilities. That's why so many people spend so much of their time teaching and coaching others. In my case, I make at least two trips per month to do just that, and that's in addition to my daily interaction with my local Consultants.

The role of "rejoice" is also confirmation that you are not alone. When others come along and openly celebrate what you have done, they too become revitalized. And rejoicing is what Mary Kay is all about. At my meetings throughout the year, as well as our company-sponsored seminar event in Dallas, we spend time rejoicing over the success of others. That may be why we are one of the most enthusiastic groups of people you will ever meet.

It's not hype . . . it's a sincere enthusiasm for the women we associate with. It is an absolute joy to be a part of this great team.

A Personal Time to Rejoice

Over the years, my biggest cheering section has been my family. My Mom and my sisters have always been interested in following my progress . . . and they rejoiced at every little success. That started when I was a little girl. Now, I want to tell you about my sister, Donna.

After having two children, Donna returned to her full-time job. Just like many of us, Donna found the stresses of trying to work full time and care for a family to be a difficult balancing act. In 1995, Donna decided to pursue her own business as a Mary Kay Independent Beauty Consultant. In the beginning, Donna was like me and so many other Beauty Consultants; she started as a part timer just to see if it was something she enjoyed.

Donna made the decision to quit her full-time job and stay home to care for her children and pursue her own business with Mary Kay. About three years after she quit her job, I was talking on the phone with Donna and I told her that we did not yet have a Sales Director in Ireland, and asked her why she did not try to be the first one. Another Irish Consultant had made the decision to become a Sales Director as well, so Donna was off and running to try to be the first. She had made the commitment. Things were going pretty well for Donna until she broke her wrist. The injury put Donna on the sidelines for a while. In the meantime, the other Consultant became the first Director in Ireland.

After she recovered from her broken wrist, Donna committed to continue her quest and become the second Sales Director in Ireland. Donna's husband and her two children became her cheering section (along with some long-distance cheering from me) and in June 2002 Donna achieved her goal. Now, Donna is the only Director in Ireland, and if I might be allowed to brag (and rejoice a little as well), she has set her goal to become the first Independent National Sales Director we've ever had in Ireland. That's something to rejoice about!

We All Want to Rejoice

When I think about my Mary Kay meetings I really get excited. We call them "Success Events." We celebrate the baby steps of a new Consultant. We also celebrate when someone becomes one of those rare National Sales Directors (we only have about 200 or so who are active in the United States). When I go to the annual meeting in Dallas, I get to observe tens of thousands of people rejoicing over the accomplishments of others. It is inspirational to watch.

I cannot imagine staying in a career where you go to work every day, do a great job, and never even hear a "well done" from the people you work with. That was my life before Mary Kay. I truly believe that rejoicing is one of the reasons so many people become inspired to go so far beyond their perceived abilities. I know it was true for me.

Don't Leave Where You Are . . . Go to Something

Wise words someone once said is that you should never leave where you are . . . you should focus on going to something. To me, that means that we do not just leave a bad job, because it is a bad job. We leave because we have found something really good to go to. You see, leaving a bad situation has a negative connotation. At the same time, going toward something that is better is extremely positive.

One of the things that astounds me is some of the Consultants who decided to leave lucrative positions with companies in order to become Mary Kay Independent Beauty Consultants. Gloria Mayfield Banks, Independent Executive National Sales Director, left her job at Harvard University after earning her MBA and serving in top corporate positions. One Consultant used her Mary Kay business to allow her to pursue her lifetime dream of working as a physician at a clinic for the poor. Those are true stories about real people. And it happens almost every day to people who discover the opportunity that a sales career can bring.

Wanda Metzger was one of those people who left a profitable career to become an Independent Beauty Consultant with Mary Kay. Wanda began her business in 1977. She had a husband in college, a young daughter, and was working full-time as a legal secretary. In a lot of ways, Wanda "had it all." She was paid extremely well at her job. But she found leaving her daughter at day care to be emotionally taxing on both of them. In addition to everything else, Wanda was pursuing her degree in business while she was managing her career, a young daughter, her household, and a full-time job.

Wanda was good enough at her job that she was doing not only her job, but she was also carrying most of the work for her boss. Wanda was so proficient at her job that the firm asked her to take on the additional responsibility of working for three executive vice presidents, and the finance officer of the firm. Although Wanda had a counterpart who was supposed to help with the expanded workload, rather than help Wanda, she spent her time working crossword puzzles and typing papers (for pay) for local law students. When Wanda complained of the excessive workload, she was told that it was not any of her business.

On an impulse, Wanda picked up the phone one day and called a Mary Kay Consultant who she didn't even know. Although Wanda used the Mary Kay products and loved them, she had never thought about a Mary Kay business of her own. The Consultant she called, Jessie Hughes Logan, offered to come to her house that night to discuss the opportunities that a Mary Kay business offered. After looking at the marketing plan that night, Wanda was convinced. When she asked her husband what he thought after Jessie left, he was really encouraging, "I just don't want one of those pink cars parked in our front drive," he teased.

In looking back, Wanda talks about just how difficult that first year was:

> Right after signing my Independent Beauty Consultant agreement, another important event occurred—I found out I was pregnant. I was working 48 hours a week, going to school two nights a week, raising my daughter, and pregnant. Unfortunately, I had morning sickness, afternoon sickness, and nighttime sickness. It was not a good time to start a business. However, since we don't have quotas, no one called to kick me out. Yea!
>
> So my first year was not really a good one. In fact, I even entertained the idea of quitting. Because I "thought" about my Mary Kay business all the time (but didn't actually work it), I didn't feel like I was making any money. At that time, everyone was talking about this "Seminar thing" in Dallas. I thought I might go check it out, use what little money I had to see Dallas, as I had never been there, and then when I came home I would quit. Well, once again God stepped in. Once at Seminar, I, of course, saw the big picture and decided to come home and go to work. The rest is history.

Like I said, we rejoice a lot at seminar, and once Wanda realized the power of rejoicing and all of the success stories she heard at our annual seminar, she was sold. I think that there is nothing more inspirational than seeing people rejoice about other people's success. I think that Wanda's words tell the story best:

The obstacles I have faced in my Mary Kay business have been the usual obstacles we all face—life! I have worked my business through working other jobs, pregnancy, babies, adolescence, and now grandchildren. At this time in my life, I am faced with being a caregiver for my aging parents. I have just been so grateful for the flexibility! There is no place I could work the hours I work, have the fun I have and make the money I do!

My Mary Kay business began in November 1977. I became a Sales Director in February 1982. I have been a Star Consultant 92 quarters. I have been in the Queen's Court of Sales eight times and the Queen's Court of Recruiting once. I have been a Double Star and Triple Star Director and have earned the use of 10 career cars—five of them the prestigious PINK CADILLACs! I currently have six first line offspring Sales Directors, three second line, one third line, one second line DIQ, and a third line DIQ. The momentum is building for us to become a National Area.

I feel so blessed to be able to work on a daily basis with women, like Gillian, who want to help mentor others to success. They are on a mission to pass on Mary Kay's dream and take others along with them. We truly are dream builders and in May Kay, all your dreams can come true if you just have the courage to pursue them!

I appreciated Wanda's comments about me, but, every day women like Wanda inspire me. I rejoice with them over their success and they inspire me to get up every day and find others with whom I can share my American dream.

Rejoice Together!

As you can see, I believe that celebrating the success of others has a powerful impact on everyone who is a part of that ceremony. I think I am probably one of the very few people in the world who can start their day with enthusiasm about their work and end the day with even more. I cannot imagine doing anything else. I don't think that I would be willing to spend my time doing something else, even if it paid me twice as much, because there is something that participating in the success of others does for your soul.

As I think about my achievements and the successes of the people I work with, my mind always wanders back to that moment when I arrived in America for that first time. As I looked out over the wing of the airplane, I saw that mighty woman, the Statue of Liberty, standing there inviting me to join those who experience the American dream. I often remember the words that are inscribed on that statue:

The New Colossus

Not like the brazen giant of Greek fame,
with conquering limbs astride from land to land;
Here at our sea-washed, sunset gates shall stand
a mighty woman with a torch, whose flame
is the imprisoned lightning, and her name
Mother of Exiles. From her beacon-hand
Glows world-wide welcome; her mild eyes command

The air-bridged harbor that twin cities frame,
"Keep, ancient lands, your storied pomp!" cries she
with silent lips. "Give me your tired, your poor,
Your huddled masses yearning to breathe free,
The wretched refuse of your teeming shore,
Send these, the homeless, tempest-tost to me,
I lift my lamp beside the golden door!"

Emma Lazarus (1849–1887)

Every time I fly into that wonderful city, I am reminded of those words and just what they have meant to my life. We are a few in comparison with the world, but among the world there is none so blessed as those of us who are allowed to live under the grace of freedom and the opportunity that this wonderful land offers. It is truly something that we can come together and rejoice about each day. There is no other place on earth like America.

An Opportunity to Rejoice

For many, the Statue of Liberty symbolizes freedom, hope, and opportunity. Like them, I came to this country with $20 in my pocket and a dream in my heart. Only in America can you truly enjoy the opportunity to rejoice in your ability to become whatever God has prepared you to be. When you get right down to it, you really rejoice with the life you lead. God bless America and the life He has given us in this great country!

Chapter 4

Reach!

I recently watched a news segment about a young football player who had been paralyzed in a football game. In this extraordinary story, the injured young man decided that despite the fact that his doctors predicted he would never walk again, he decided that he would.

The footage showed the young man, now in his early twenties—walking. In spite of his prognosis, the young man decided to reach for the impossible, or at least what most thought was impossible.

What Does It Mean to "Reach"?

The concept of *reaching* has to do with setting goals that appear to be beyond your capabilities. I used the word *appear* because the goals are often not beyond your capabilities at all. If he did not reach for what appeared impossible, that young athlete might have spent his entire life in a wheelchair, never discovering that he was able to walk. Most of us are like that young man. We have things in our lives that "appear" to be impossible, but in reality they are not.

I am fortunate that in my work, I get to associate daily with women who have gone beyond their apparent limitations to become phenomenally successful. Reaching beyond what you perceive as your limitations is not just a financial limit. When you decide to reach beyond what you think you can do, your life is changed in every way.

When I first came to America, like so many before me, I came to this country with little money and a dream. But, as I slowly discovered, that was not all I had. I had the ability to set my goals beyond my own expectations. I decided to reach beyond the childhood challenges of my life in Ireland. I believe that is another important key to accomplishing anything worthwhile in life. If you compare the top salespeople in Mary Kay Inc. with those who are not successful, almost always the difference is their commitment to reach.

Once you have set your goals, to reach beyond your limitations you must visualize yourself achieving your goals. Some women anticipate being rejected even before they walk into a sales call. Others see themselves as positive people who can do whatever they decide to accomplish. That's what reach is all about.

The women figure skaters who compete in the Olympics usually go through a visualization process.

Olympic skaters often start out at a young age as part of a large group of girls. In some cases, it becomes immediately apparent that many of the skaters, both those who are gifted and those who are not, actually have little desire to be an Olympian. There are some in the group who go forward because of peer pressures or family pressures, but they usually drop out at some point. The ones who remain and go on to compete see themselves differently. They begin to see themselves as champions.

When young skaters see videos of themselves skating, they discover that their posture is not so good and the jumps they thought were so high . . . well, they're not very high at all. Rather than become discouraged, the skaters who see themselves as champions continue to watch the best competitors. They develop mental pictures of how these champions carry themselves and how they execute their jumps. After a while, the young skaters' posture and jumps change, and they begin to look more like the Olympic skaters they have been watching. Once they commit to seeing themselves in terms of what they could become, they start reaching for higher accomplishments. The farther you reach, the greater your successes will be.

My Early Inspiration

Not too long after I began my own Mary Kay business, I heard a speech by a woman named Rena Tarbet. I had attended a sales conference and Rena had given a three-hour class. Rena has been selling Mary Kay products for 37 years. For many of those years, she has been driving a pink Cadillac. She has been recognized so many times for many personal accomplishments, it would be difficult to include them all in this short chapter. Rena is one of those people who define *reach*.

But there is a lot more to Rena's story. Rena's married life began under pretty difficult circumstances. Her husband was a counselor for abused children, but was paid so little that he and his new wife had to live in government housing for the first few years of their marriage. Rena decided that she had to help in getting her husband and three children out of subsidized housing into better conditions. She discovered the Mary Kay opportunity and immediately recognized that it was the one opportunity that she had seen that allowed her to determine what her earnings would be. Once she realized that her success or failure was up to her, Rena began reaching for her dream. It was not long before the family was able to move out of the subsidized housing and into a house of their own.

Then 27 years ago, Rena encountered a challenge that threatened not only her business, but also her life. Rena's doctor discovered that she had breast cancer. Rena underwent chemotherapy and radiation to battle the disease. Never one to give up, Rena has survived a number of recurrences of her cancer over the years, but she maintains that she has a lot of things that she still wants to accomplish in her life and cancer is not in her plans.

Rena has a favorite saying, "Every experience in life makes you better or bitter . . . It's your choice." I want you to think about this: Rena has endured nine years of chemotherapy, 60 series of radiation treatments, and 19 surgeries in the past 27 years. While she was going through all of that, she had the top-performing unit in all of Mary Kay. She then became an Independent National Sales Director.

Can you imagine going from living in subsidized housing to having your own neighborhood? That's exactly what Rena did. She bought a large parcel of land outside of Fort Worth, Texas, and built her dream house. Her plans were not limited to her dream house, she always wanted to live near her children, so one by one as the houses nearby came up for sale, her children purchased the homes and moved in. That's where they all live today, right there in Rena's "neighborhood." Rena's husband of 43 years is still a counselor with the same agency that he was with when they got married. He still spends his time working with abused children.

At one of our annual events called Seminars, I had the opportunity to room with Rena. Every morning she got up and took all of the medications for her cancer, and then got ready to teach a class at Seminar. As we walked out of our room that first morning, Rena looked at me and said, "Let's go show these people how they can change the rest of their lives!"

It is perhaps that one statement that gave me insight into Rena's soul. Her entire life has been all about helping others. In order to do that, Rena had to overcome odds that would have overwhelmed most, but Rena is one of those inspirational people who reach beyond their circumstances to achieve their dreams. Rena, by the way, comes by her inspiration the old fashioned way. A committed Christian, Rena believes that God has carried her through all of these years, and the only time she's supposed to give up is when He decides its time.

Teaching Others to Reach

Kaye Hemphill is one of those people who live by the principles of *reach* every day. Kaye moved from Atlanta, Georgia, to Edmond, Oklahoma, over 25 years ago. With two children under the age of 2, Kaye was not sure she wanted to go back to work. Kaye was a schoolteacher who loved her students, but really wanted to be able to stay at home and care for her own children. She decided to accept a substitute teaching position. After two days, Kaye decided that was not for her. From there, she tried working at a daycare center, with about the same results.

Kaye wanted to be free to be with her children during the day and simply did not like the restrictions that full-time work put on her. One day a few years ago, Kaye was invited to attend a Mary Kay meeting. She was so excited about the opportunity to sell Mary Kay products that she signed up 24 hours later. Shortly after signing up, she realized there was a problem with her new endeavor. Kaye had recently moved and did not know many people in her new city. After a bit of coaching from her fellow consultants and her Sales Director, Kaye began reaching out, first to her family, then to her neighbors and the few acquaintances she had made. She also decided to attend various functions that would allow her to meet more people. At one such event, Kaye walked away with over 30 prospective customers.

Kaye admits that starting her Mary Kay business was a big reach. Aside from being new to the town she lived in, Kaye was also somewhat shy and introverted when she first began her sales career. Although she was a teacher, she was still uncomfortable speaking in front of groups and was reluctant to strike up conversations with new people.

Over time, Kaye grew as a person as well as a sales professional. She saw in her fellow Consultants skills and abilities she wanted to emulate, and focused on seeing herself as a successful salesperson, rather than the shy, introverted person she always thought she was. No longer hesitant to meet new people, she began to see strangers as new friends that she "just had not met yet." Kaye is one of those people who understand what it means to reach to create opportunity where there appears to be none. Kaye became a Mary Kay Independent Sales Director just 15 months after becoming a Beauty Consultant. Sixteen months after that, she earned the use of her first car.

Kaye recently wrote and told me how important her Mary Kay business has been to her. She told me about how she had earned the use of 14 cars as well as the other awards and prizes she had received. Of all of the bonuses she has earned, the best gift she received during her life is being able to live her dream of staying at home with her children while continuing her business. "Obviously, I love the sales business and dealing with people. I'm truly happy. I never had to go back to the classroom except as a mommy."

Kaye is a lot like so many successful sales people that I have the joy of working with. I think that the most exciting thing about my work is not the financial opportunity that I have, it's the *people opportunity* that I have. I get to see people like Kaye achieve things that they never thought possible. It all comes down to convincing people to reach for the stars. They already have the ability; it's just getting them to make the commitment. I get to rejoice every day as I see ordinary people achieving extraordinary feats.

Inspired to Reach

Kaye told me about one of the Consultants in her sales unit who had been an inspiration to her. One day Kaye was on the phone with one of her Mary Kay Consultants named Janis Clemens. In the middle of their conversation, Janis stopped talking and said, sobbing, "I think my husband is dead."

Kaye tells of how she raced over to Janis's house, only to find emergency responders wheeling Janis's husband out to a waiting ambulance parked in front of the house. At the young age of 27, Janis's husband had died of a heart attack. Janis was left to care for her small daughter alone.

Janis worked as a registered nurse, but the idea of leaving her daughter at day care so that she could work did not appeal to her. She felt that she needed to be home with her, especially since the little girl had just lost her father. Janis decided to make the commitment of her life, she decided to leave her job as a nurse and pursue her Mary Kay business so she could stay at home with her child. To some, leaving a steady income and the security nursing offered would have been unthinkable. Janis knew that she wanted more but to get it she had to step outside of her comfort zone into uncertain waters. She decided to reach. That was in 1983, and since then Janis has achieved numerous goals, won many awards, and has driven a pink Cadillac for a long time.

Many people might have tried to convince Janis that the "safe decision" for her was to go back to nursing. But with a young daughter, a job that required night and weekend shifts, Janis made the decision to reach for her dreams. She wanted to be able to care for her young child and at the same time needed to earn a living. By reaching for her dreams, Janis was able to achieve her goals.

Winning

Even the top sales professionals are successful only about 20 percent of the time. That means they have to see their way past 80 percent rejections to get to the 20 percent of the customers who will buy. If you commit to a sales profession, you must be capable of seeing past the rejections and focus on the successes. Some people have difficulty doing that. If you are committed to reaching beyond your perceived ability, you must accept the fact that not everyone will buy. That may be the most challenging aspect of reaching. The question you are probably asking is this: If I commit to reaching, how can I learn to think differently about myself and my abilities? How can I learn to look past those moments of failure and focus on the times in which I enjoy success? How can I learn to become someone who achieves things that I do not think I can?

My answer to these questions is simple: Work with someone who does it. As a Mary Kay Independent Beauty Consultant, I am fortunate to be associated with many women who fit this description. Mary Kay Inc. has a tradition of mentoring that goes all the way back to the company's founder, Mary Kay Ash. One of the remarkable things about the company is just how many people are willing to teach another person how to exceed her expectations of herself. Of course, what follows is success.

Here is my challenge for you: Look for the most professional salesperson you can find and work with them. Just like the skater who watches an Olympic champion so she can learn, you too need to watch an Olympic "sales" champion so you can understand how that person learned to achieve excellence. More often than not (in fact, in almost every case), you will find that they had the same feelings of inadequacy about themselves as you are experiencing.

With that recommendation comes a word of caution: I have observed many sales people who try to copy the personality of another salesperson. That is not what I am referring to. What I recommend is observing and understanding their attitude, their work habits, and how they deal with people. You can be successful without changing who you are. You do not need to become someone different or copy someone else's sales approach. In fact, if you do that, you will not be successful. If you are to become a success, you have to be you and no one else. I know some sales professionals who are great comedians. That's not me. At the same time, I have realized that I have an enthusiasm for people and I want others to succeed. I allow my natural gifts to carry me. That's how I can work toward being the person that I believe I am capable of being.

Starting at the Bottom

Every time I go to a sales meeting I hear different success stories. At one recent meeting, there was a young, shy college student named Lauren. To the average observer, it would not appear that she was your typical sales dynamo.

It turns out that the young college student was the daughter of a woman who had been an Independent Beauty Consultant for a number of years. As a teenager, Lauren had informed her mother that she wanted to have her own Mary Kay business. Lauren's demeanor was extremely well suited to a sales career. She was pleasant and persistent in working with her customers.

Under that quiet demeanor was a winner. Lauren was able to use her business to support herself all through college. She was already achieving her goals while attending the university full time and expected to graduate from college with a thriving business. It really has nothing to do with where you start. It's all about where you finish.

What about You?

So far I have been talking about other people. The question is: What about you? What best describes you? Are you committed to mediocrity, or are you determined to discover the winner inside yourself as did Kaye and Janis? Chances are, you have the ability to achieve exceptional goals. The question is whether you are willing to seek the very best for yourself. So the question remains: What about you? Are you ready to make the commitment?

Reaching for the Stars

I propose the following challenge: Write down three goals or dreams that you believe are out of your reach. Now, I want to introduce you to a concept called *chipping*. Chipping is a technique that wise people use to reach beyond their perceived abilities. You don't focus on the big goal, but you chip away at it. You set up a road map of goals. Then you stay on the path. More importantly, if you set your goals up correctly, you will find that reaching for the stars involves little more than recognizing your dream and committing to small steps each day.

Respect, Reach, and Rejoice!

I hope that the stories of these incredible women have touched your life as they have touched mine. Success is about more than money or status. Success is about all of the people whose lives you can touch and inspire to reach beyond their perceived abilities.

PART III

The Ten Principles for Sales Success

Chapter 5

Think Like a Champion

It has been said that perception is everything. How we perceive ourselves directly influences our choices and behaviors. This is the difference between people who win in life and those who do not. Usually, people who do not succeed at reaching the goals they set perceive themselves as failures before they even try. When a new Consultant joins my team, one of the first things I want to know is how they see themselves. If they believe they are unqualified or incompetent, that's exactly how they will perform.

Often, my first goal is to help them discover the champion inside.

In the previous chapter, I talked about how important it is for each of us to make the commitment to reach beyond our perceived abilities. Once you have made that commitment, you need to change how you act. To change how you act, you must change how you think, because "how you think is how you act."

How many times have you met someone who was extremely talented but never did anything about it because they did not see themselves as capable? When you look back to your school experiences, do you see classmates who graduated to mediocrity? Do you remember those people you came into contact with who were so committed to failure, whether they realized it or not, that nothing could change their course?

Commitment to success or failure, whether conscious or unconscious, influences all of our thoughts and actions once the commitment has been made. If you commit to thinking like a failure, you will fail. In fact, if you focus entirely on your inabilities, you are guaranteed to fail. Further, if you think what you can achieve is limited by the events that happened in your life and what you perceive as your abilities, you will also fail. How you think affects everything else in your life.

I want to make sure that you do not get the wrong idea. I do not believe that you can necessarily become a brain surgeon. Success is not simply a matter of visualizing a goal and waiting for it to happen. Success is more about realizing your true potential. If you lack the talent, the physical skills, and the mental capacity to be a brain surgeon, no amount of mental "tricks" will enable you to be a brain surgeon.

Let's be honest about most people: From childhood, many people are taught to think of themselves in certain ways. As we grow up, whether our experiences are good or bad, we learn about how others think we should think of ourselves. For example, if a man is short and, as a youth, everyone around him tells him that he is limited in life because he is short, then more often than not he will grow up believing he is limited because he is short. Sadly, that often carries over to everything a person believes about himself.

What Is Your Script?

My childhood with an alcoholic father had a significant impact on my life. My nanny Mae also had an impact on me. Of course, my mother was a constant in my life, always counseling me and teaching me how to think about myself. Much like actors, people have a script that seems to drive the way they think and act. When I combine all these different influences on my life, by the time I was 18, I already had an internal script that determined how I thought as well as how I behaved.

Sometimes the scripts developed during your childhood are not positive scripts. Many of us are like that young injured football player in the last chapter. He was told that he was going to spend the rest of his life in a wheelchair. He had the ability to walk, but only because he decided to get out of the wheelchair. The same is true of self-defeating scripts. Unless you decide to become the person you really are and not the one you were taught to think you are, the false script will control your life.

For a moment, think about three people you know who have not achieved their potential in life. Now, see if you can give a name to the script that each one is living out. For example, I know someone who is very critical of other people. It destroys her relationships. It might be fair to say that her script might be called "I'm angry." Often, critical people are angry with themselves or another in their life that they cannot express their anger to, and that is why they go around making others angry by criticizing them.

I know another person who, when faced with a task or challenge, responds by saying, "I can't do that." Her life is a series of comments about what she cannot do. I would call her script "I'm a failure."

People with scripts like "I'm angry" and "I'm a failure" will have a difficult time succeeding in life. By allowing their scripts to control their lives, they are setting themselves up to fail. Down deep, they truly believe that they are unworthy of success. That is where changing the way you think comes in. Once you have *reached* by setting life goals that appear to be out of your realm of possibility. You have to accomplish one more step: You have to realize that you need to think about yourself differently. You need to learn to change your script so that you *think like a champion.*

Thinking like a champion involves recognizing your God-given talents and making the commitment to maximize them. A salesperson, who usually finishes in the bottom half of her group in one setting, will almost always finish in the bottom half of any group she joins. The problem is that she is not ready to succeed. Her script is leading her toward failure.

The Story of Susan and Jane

Susan has been working in sales for a few years, but has never done very well. She works the "program" she was taught during her orientation and she does it well. She calls a certain number of potential clients every day but she struggles to get the same number of appointments that her peers do. Susan is a low performer.

Since her childhood, Susan was told that she did not have good interpersonal skills. She believed that lesson and has spent her entire life living out that belief. As she prepares to make her calls each day, Susan does not see herself as a successful salesperson. In fact, she sees just the opposite. When she is successful, she attributes it to good luck. Susan sees herself as a failure and is devoted to living out that script in her life. With that attitude, Susan will consistently fail.

Jane, on the other hand, sees herself as a champion. Ironically, Jane had about the same upbringing as Susan but along the way something happened to Jane. Jane encountered many of the same life challenges as Susan did, but unlike Susan, Jane decided to breakthrough instead of breakdown. Jane decided to take her future in her own hands and learn to live differently. Although on the outside, Jane appeared to lack many of the talents that Susan possessed, Jane became much more successful. Jane had begun to think like a champion.

In building my business, I have observed that the major difference between the high achievers and the low achievers is not where they start, it's where they decide to finish. You need to have the basic talent to succeed, but most people have that talent. The problem is, like Susan, most people are committed to failing rather than to succeeding.

What about You?

So far I have been talking about other people. What about you? Who best describes you? Are you committed to mediocrity like Susan or are you determined to discover the champion inside like Jane? Chances are, you have the ability to achieve exceptional goals. The only question is whether or not you are willing to seek the very best for yourself. So the issue is: What about you? Are you ready to make the decision to succeed and commit to visualizing yourself as a champion?

I Want to Be Better Than Sammy Sosa!

A few years ago, I met a man named Albert Pujols. At that time, Albert was dating De De Corona, one of my relatives, and we would occasionally meet at family functions. Albert had come to America as an immigrant, just like I had. Albert had come to Kansas City from the Dominican

Republic. As a child, he played baseball using a stick as a bat, a baseball made of tape, and a milk carton for a baseball glove. For many children in the Dominican Republic, baseball is their only way of dreaming to escape poverty.

By the time he came to the United States at age 16, Albert had a dream of playing baseball at the professional level. When I met him, I could see that all 6 feet 3 inches of him was committed to that dream. Although Albert was a really gentle and considerate man on the outside, inside there was a burning desire to play professional baseball.

I had a chance to talk with Albert at a family function one evening. I asked him if he had dreams of being just like Sammy Sosa. "Oh no" he replied, "I want to be better than Sammy Sosa." I often tell people that God never gives you a dream unless He already has a plan for you to fulfill it. That turned out to be true in the life of Albert Pujols.

When Albert's family arrived in the United States, they settled in New York. After Albert witnessed a killing, his grandmother insisted that they move out of the city and the family decided to move to Independence, Missouri. There, Albert entered high school and began learning English and playing on the school baseball team. Albert turned out to be a coach's dream. He hit better than .500 with 11 home runs in his first season playing. Even today, his former coach tells of the day that Albert hit a 450-foot home run that landed on top of an air conditioner that was 25 feet high.

The team's opponents were none too happy about the newfound talent of the team. The next season, Albert was intentionally walked 55 times in 88 times at bat. He did manage to hit eight home runs and receive state all-star honors that season. As a result of his high school successes, the baseball coach at Maple Woods Community College recruited Albert.

It was about that time that Albert met 21-year-old De De Corona. He met her at a nightclub and passed himself off as being 21 instead of 18, his actual age. But De De had a secret of her own. When Albert finally confessed his real age to her, she shared her secret with him. She had a young daughter who had been diagnosed with Down Syndrome.

Most men of Albert's age would have walked away from such a responsibility. Instead, Albert continued to get to know De De and her daughter better and came to love them both a great deal.

In his 1999 season at Maple Woods, Albert had a great year. His batting average that year was .461 and he hit 22 home runs. The St. Louis Cardinals offered Albert a contract and a $10,000 signing bonus. Not satisfied with the offer, Albert instead decided to play for a Kansas minor league team called the Hays Larks. Albert had an exceptional year that year and the Cardinals again offered him a contract, this time with a signing bonus of $60,000. He accepted their offer and that winter Albert and De De were married. The Cardinals assigned Albert to their minor league team, the Peoria Chiefs, for the 2000 season. It was in Peoria that Albert moved from shortstop to third base. Again, Albert was successful that season.

As he began the 2001 spring training season, Albert was supposed to be assigned to the Cardinals' AAA farm team. But Albert's play during spring training and an injury to one of the Cardinals team members opened the door for Albert to make the 2001 Cardinals major league team. That year, instead of warming the bench, Albert worked his way into the starting lineup. He not only made the National League All-Star team, but hit a very respectable .329, and that included 37 home runs and 47 doubles, making him the first baseball player in history with a .300 batting average, more than 30 home runs, and 100 runs batted in. He was named the National League Rookie of the Year.[1]

A Winner and a Teacher

One day after high school baseball practice, my son Vince Jr. came home completely discouraged. Knowing that Vince had aspirations of being a professional baseball player, two students had jokingly said he would never play baseball anywhere else except high school. Their taunting really had an impact on him.

I called Albert and asked if he would mind talking with Vince Jr. I felt that he needed to understand just how hard Albert worked to make it to the Major Leagues, how he did not let others' opinions of him stop him, and how he had to let go of his fear of failing. One thing he told Vince was

[1] Jockbio.com.

that he had to see himself as bigger than those kids who had made fun of him. What he was really saying is "you have to see the champion inside of you." Over time, Albert continued to spend time with Vince and I could see just how valuable Albert's encouragement was.

When Vince Jr. was a senior in high school, he applied to enter Maple Woods Community College, the same one that Albert had attended. Vince also made the baseball team his senior year. During that year, Vince dislocated his hip. With Albert's continued encouragement, he was able to come back from that injury. During his recuperation, Albert continued to encourage Vince to think about playing at Maple Woods Community College. Albert's encouragement made a real difference in Vince's life. Today, Vince Jr. happily plays for Maple Woods and is now looking forward to making the team at a four-year college next year.

What Is Holding YOU Back?

There is no amount of positive thinking that will overcome an absence of talent. The problem is most of us have a lot more talent than we think we do. Fear of failure is probably the most driving force in the lives of most people. Can you imagine going through life with an awesome gift or talent and never discovering it?

When he was a child, Enrico Caruso's parents took him to a music teacher who auditioned him and assessed his singing talent. The teacher told Enrico's parents that

Enrico had no talent, and that they certainly should not encourage him to continue singing.[2] Despite this edict, the world has been blessed by the phenomenal voice of Enrico Caruso. What would have happened if Enrico Caruso had not decided to discover the champion in himself? What will happen to you if you do not make that same decision?

Changed Lives

One of the joys of my life is meeting and interacting with all of the people who find Mary Kay. Some say they just want to make a few extra dollars. Others say they got involved to please a friend. What happens after that is inspirational. I see thousands of women discover "the champion within." I see lives changed.

[2] *Kindred Spirit,* vol. 22, no. 3 (Autumn 1998).

Chapter 6

Discipline Creates Excellence

The old adage, "Plan your work and work your plan," is extremely relevant in business, but it is especially true for sales. These simple words contain sound advice. I've spent a lot of time speaking about the idea of reaching for the future, now I want to tell you what it takes to execute your plans and dreams.

One of the first things I had to learn about selling was that it required discipline. At the time I entered the direct-selling business full time, I had a young son and a husband to care for. In looking at my personal priorities, God, Family, Career, I realized that I had to learn to set daily goals and priorities in each area of my life if I was to be successful. Obviously, my day had to begin with getting Vince and Vince Jr. out of the house. That was not always easy. As a police officer, Vince often worked early or late depending on his assignments.

The last thing I did each evening was to plan my next day. I sat down and figured out what I had to do from a time management standpoint to take care of the family issues I had to deal with. Once I had a plan for that, I was then ready to plan my workday. I knew that I had to reach a certain activity level each day if I was to meet my sales goals. One way to make sure you are disciplined is to actually write down your plan for the day. Let's take a look at how I did that for my particular situation:

6:00 A.M. to 8:00 A.M. Prepare breakfast, pack lunches, drive Vince Jr. to school.

8:00 A.M. to 10:00 A.M. Do grocery/cleaners run on the way home, wash clothes, clean house.

10:00 A.M. to 12:00 noon Make prospect calls for new customers and follow up calls with a daily goal of at least five new customer calls per day.

12:00 noon to 1:30 P.M. Initiate new business activities, go to lunch with a prospect, attend networking meetings, engage in other activities where I would meet new people.

1:30 P.M. to 3:00 P.M. Make new business calls/presentations.

3:00 P.M. to 6:00 P.M. Family time; have dinner ready for Vince when he gets off work.

After 6:00 P.M. Plan my next day, finish orders, paperwork, and so on.

In addition, I usually have meetings scheduled a couple of evenings each week, plus I almost always have one meeting scheduled on Saturday. I also travel and speak about two weekends per month. Even though I'm running a fairly large business, I still make sure I have time allocated for new contacts. I've noticed over the years that the top sales professionals never stop working on new business. That seems to be the rule for long-term success.

Some Have Excuses . . . Others Have Reasons

When it comes to self-discipline, I have noticed that there are people out there who are looking for an excuse to fail. If you ask them why they have never been successful, you might hear some of the following reasons:

- My parents never taught me to be disciplined.
- I'm disorganized . . . that's just the way I am.
- I have a learning disability.
- I simply have too much to do.
- Something always seems to get in the way.
- I'm just not a good salesperson, I guess.

Let me make one thing clear: Those are excuses. Most of the successful people I know can also point to one or more of those issues and tell you that describes them and they still go on to be successful despite their shortcomings. So . . . what's the deal?

When was the last time you traveled and gave a presentation when you were running a fever? When was the last time you made a presentation when you had one of those "near migraine" headaches? People who allow excuses to run their lives don't make it to those presentations. People with reasons . . . made just about every one of them. Those who have a reason to succeed get the job done. Those who live a life characterized by allowing excuses to justify their failure never get to the top. Winners have purpose in their lives. They have a reason behind their behavior. It is who they are. They are disciplined and that means they are unwilling to allow anything to stand between them and a commitment that they have made to another individual.

Some People Have Reasons

I have seen many people start with nothing to become phenomenally successful. In every case, they made a conscious decision to overcome something. In other words, they had a reason to succeed. Achieving success is a lot like walking . . . you can only take one step at a time to get there. When people decide that they are going to personally take charge of their lives, they have to do it one step . . . and one decision at a time. That is what discipline is. But there is more.

Have you ever known someone who went on a diet only to quit dieting after giving in to a piece of chocolate cake? Again, that minor infraction is just an excuse. Discipline is a commitment to a way of life. When you commit to being a disciplined person, it means that you have committed to being a different person. Okay, so you had that piece of chocolate cake. You have to look at yourself in the mirror and say, "I made a mistake . . . but that's not who I am anymore!" Discipline is a commitment to be different. It is a commitment to taking charge of your own life and your own future.

A Written Plan for Success

I have a friend who was given the challenge of turning around a difficult sales territory. After a lot of thinking, he decided that all he could do was face the challenge one day at a time. Each day, he targeted the new business calls that he knew he had to make to be successful. He ended each day by making a list of the 10 prospect calls (names and phone numbers) that he was going to start the next day with. He knew that if he did not make those 10 calls each morning, he was going to fail. He took the territory from a huge loss position to profitability within 120 days. That's what discipline is. You have to start each day with a written plan for success and implement that plan.

Another great thing about a written plan is that it allows you to keep track of all of the contacts you have made. If you keep good notes, you can call an old contact back just to follow up with them and make sure they know that you are still there. As I have learned, things can change over time and what used to be a cold prospect can turn into a hot lead.

Robin Wood: Discipline for Winning

I first met Robin Wood when she became an Independent Beauty Consultant in 2001. Robin is one of those people who seem to always have it all together. In the beginning, Robin had no intention of starting her own business. After all, she had a secure corporate job and was well thought of by the people in her company.

Robin and her husband were married at the age of 21. They were prudent with their financial affairs. In order to afford the house they wanted, they were willing to drive older automobiles and to carefully plan their spending. A few years after they married, they had two children.

One day a friend invited Robin to have a complimentary facial so she could show her the Mary Kay products. "I absolutely loved the product," said Robin. Robin also became fascinated with the idea of selling the product. She expressed her interest to her friend. Not long after that, she signed her Mary Kay Independent Beauty Consultant agreement.

"You've got to understand," said Robin, "I never intended to go into business for myself. I just loved selling the product. I had a wonderful job, I loved the company, and loved my work." It seems that Robin had a gift for sales. After becoming a Consultant in February 2001, she earned the use of a career car in only eight months. That's quite an accomplishment for a Consultant after only eight months of effort.

"You can't believe what it meant to me," said Robin. "I was driving a 1987 car. The career car was the first new car I had ever driven in my life." Robin loved selling and she loved enjoying the fruits of her labor.

It was at about that time that Robin decided to tell her husband about the investment she had made in inventory after she became an Independent Consultant. "When I first told him I was going to sell Mary Kay products he was not real excited. I didn't tell him I had gone to my company credit union and borrowed a few thousand dollars to buy inventory," said Robin. "By the time I got the car, he was already impressed with the extra money I was making. I felt I could tell him about it then, especially since I had already sold out my inventory a number of times over that eight-month period."

It became apparent that Robin was on the fast track to success. She went on to achieve the status of Independent Sales Director in only one year from the date that she became a Consultant.

I asked Robin about how she was able to achieve so much in such a short period of time. I thought it was especially notable that she had done it while working full time plus having a family of four to care for. "It's all about decisions and discipline," said Robin. She went on to explain that the key was making the decision to achieve specific goals. Then she exercised the discipline by executing a specific plan that ensured her success. "Early on I figured out that sales success is all about planning your activities," said Robin. "I made sure that I was diligent in meeting my planned goals each week. The good news about our products is that if you make enough contacts each week, the product is good enough that the customers are sold."

Struggles along the Way

I did not know of Robin's struggles during this time. Robin is the type of person who works to overcome obstacles and rarely discuss them. Robin's young son had become very ill. The doctors could not figure out why. After visiting many different doctors, she took him to a physician that specialized in chronic diseases. Her son was diagnosed with Lyme disease. Typically contracted through ticks, Lyme disease displays symptoms similar to other autoimmune diseases.

It turned out that Robin's daughter had the disease as well. Both of Robin's children had to undergo extensive treatment for the disease. As if she did not have enough to deal with, in February 2003 Robin came down with mononucleosis and pneumonia. Her doctor became suspicious and tested Robin for Lyme disease. The diagnosis was not good. Robin had two different strains of Lyme disease and had probably had it since she was around seven years old. It became apparent that her children had contracted the disease from Robin even though the disease had been dormant all those years.

"We were involved in a major project at work," said Robin. "Worse yet, I was responsible for coordinating a lot of the work. I was really discouraged. I found that the real problem I was having was more about Lyme disease than it was the mono or the pneumonia." Robin also began having problems speaking (a side effect of the disease). That was a problem for her at work, since she had to speak to groups on a frequent basis. One of the commitments that Robin had made was that she wanted to earn the use of a pink Cadillac in 2003. In spite of working at a full-time job and dealing with her illness, Robin "worked her plan" to earn the use of a Cadillac. In March 2003, Robin earned her pink Cadillac. "I drove it to work," she said. "That was a proud moment for me, in spite of all of the difficulties I had encountered."

Even though Robin had gone through numerous treatments, one of the strains of the disease that Robin had would not respond to treatment. "Thankfully," she said, "my children did not get that strain of the disease." With her children on the mend and a pink Cadillac in her garage, it looked like Robin was on track to have a great 2004. By the end of 2003, however, it became apparent that the treatments were simply not working, and her symptoms again became pronounced.

"I had been on as many as three powerful antibiotics all at one time," said Robin. In March of 2004, Robin informed her company that she had to take a medical leave. Although she was going through a really traumatic time, Robin again used her approach to personal discipline to make sure that she kept her Mary Kay sales on track. In June of 2004, she informed her company that she was resigning due to her illness. Robin continues to spend thousands of dollars on medical treatment, and hopes in the near future to find an effective treatment. "In the meantime," she says, "I've replaced my corporate income with my personal Mary Kay sales. Thanks to a great team of supporters, I truly believe I can get through all of this. I owe it all to the Mary Kay career opportunity."

Discipline Creates Excellence

I am so proud of Robin and especially the way she has persevered despite the challenges she has faced. I hope you realize just how critical discipline is when it comes to excellence. It is not the gigantic achievements that lead to a successful sales career. It is the daily discipline . . . the accomplishing of those little steps each day that lead to gigantic accomplishments.

As a Christian, I often read scriptures that talk about how I am to "walk." When you think about it, that is what success of any type is all about. It's the decision to take one step at a time. Each step leads you closer and closer to your goal. When you have to climb up an impossible mountain, it can only be done by focusing on one step at a time. One step at a time . . . that's discipline.

As I have the opportunity to get to know different groups of salespeople around the country, I find that figuring out which ones are going to do well is really easy. Most of them have dreams, but a few have a plan. The few that have a plan know what they are going to achieve each day. They are disciplined. Those people stand out in a crowd. It is a joy for me to go back a year or two later and meet with the same group of people. In just about every case, those who were committed to personal discipline are those who achieved excellence.

What about you? Have you thought about your dreams? Have you given up on achieving them because they are too big for you to achieve? I want to challenge you today to commit to living the life of discipline. Plan each day and work your plan each day. That is when you will discover just how capable and gifted you really are.

Chapter 7

I Can!

As I look back on my life, I realize that at some point my personality changed from that of an "I can't!" person to an " I can!" person. I believe that the saying: "Defeat has not occurred until you quit" is a strong and poignant one. Do you realize just how true that is? My problem with the "I can't!" way of living is that the people who believe they can't rarely ever go out to play the game of life. They rather hide in the safety of their " I can't!" beliefs and never take the chance to succeed. That's where I was a number of years ago when I met Independent National Sales Director Cathy Bill-Malpica.

I believe I am a very good judge of character, but sometimes I almost subconsciously make snap judgments about people, and those judgments are wrong. When I first saw Cathy Bill-Malpica, I made one of those judgments, but it did not take long for me to change my mind. When many of us think of successful people, especially women, we often have a mental picture of a tall, slender woman, dressed in a Brooks Brothers suit, standing in the board room of a company. At barely five feet tall, Cathy does not immediately tower over the people she meets. It does not, however, take long for you to realize that Cathy is an accomplished person who almost demands your attention by her very presence. When Cathy enters a room, she exudes confidence. You immediately realize that Cathy is one of the most successful sales professionals you will every meet.

In this chapter, I'm going to tell you about how five-foot-tall 200 plus-pound Cathy worked her plan to lose more than half that weight. Accomplishing the goal of weight loss despite the amount of time, willpower, and commitment it takes is an example of success most everyone can relate to. Cathy did not lose all that weight at one time. She lost it one pound at a time. That is a really important concept to understand. We reach our goals by accomplishing one small step at a time. If we only look at the top of the mountain we have to climb, we will usually become discouraged even before we begin. The key is to look at the first step, then the second, and then the next step . . . all the way to the top.

Cathy was not raised in a wealthy family nor was she sent to the best schools. Prior to 1987, Cathy was a young married woman who took a series of dead-end jobs including chopping onions for a hot dog vendor and working as an apartment cleaner. She even worked as a gas station attendant. Some people do a series of dead-end jobs until they reach their life's end, but not Cathy Bill-Malpica.

Cathy Bill-Malpica, for all of the challenges that she experienced while growing up, had one thing going for her that would make all the difference in the world. Cathy had a mother who taught her the lesson of "I can!" Cathy's mother raised her to believe that she was a capable, competent individual, even though Cathy had been categorized as having a learning disability while in school.

The first time I saw her, Cathy walked into the room with such confidence that you absolutely knew that you had to listen to her. As she spoke, I realized that Cathy, despite her humble beginnings, had already had a career of record-breaking performance and accomplishments. After becoming a member of the Mary Kay independent sales force, Cathy set out to become an Independent National Sales Director. In order to achieve that goal, Cathy had to be not only a great producer, but she had to be able to convince others to believe in themselves. She had to convince a lot of people to change their opinions of themselves from " I can't!" to "I can!"

From "I Can't!" to "I Can!"

Listening to Cathy talk that day, I found it almost unbelievable that she had come so far. As I watched this slim five-foot-tall dynamo tell the rest of her story, I was amazed. Cathy had not only been through one dead-end job after another for a number of years, at one time she had tipped the scales at over 300 pounds! This woman had not only demonstrated a change to an "I can!" attitude, she had made "I can!" a way of life. That was my introduction to Cathy Bill-Malpica.

Little did I realize how much impact she would have on my own life. By the time I had met Cathy, I had worked my way up the career path and had been somewhat successful in recruiting. As I sat in the back of the room that day, I distinctly remember Cathy telling the group that she was personally willing to teach us how we could also achieve our dreams and goals. I believe it was that moment that crystallized my personal dream for success. I realized that I was earning money, but it wasn't really a thriving business yet. Most of all, I realized that I was being given the opportunity to live what I call the "Amer-I Can!" dream. It's just that I had not yet made the commitment to move to the point in my life where I was willing to live "I can!" That day as I listened to Cathy, I made the commitment.

The Five Characteristics of "I Can't!" People

It might be accurate to say that commitment is the mother of success. If you are unwilling to commit to being successful, it is likely that you will fail. Committing to success begins with saying "I can!" I want to describe the people I have encountered who live on the "I can't!" side of life. The first thing I want you to realize is that they are no different than the people who live on the "I can!" side of the tracks. They have the same abilities and potential. The only difference is, they have chosen to live on the "I can't!" side of the tracks instead of the "I can!" side of the tracks. Here is what I most commonly see in those "I can't!" people:

1. They are overwhelmed by their past failures.
2. They begin every day with an "I can't!" attitude.
3. They fail because they never begin to succeed.
4. They believe they are victims, not victors.
5. They are unquestionably committed to fail.

One of the most interesting things I have realized about "I can't!" people is that they often dream of being successful and of having a happy life. The problem is they are unwilling or don't know how to get started and succeed.

Five Steps to Becoming an "I Can!" Person

One of the most discouraging things that happens to people is that they are trapped in a cycle of not knowing how to become successful, and failing when they try. If you want to become successful in sales, you have to be someone who can rejoice in the 20 percent of the presentations in which you are successful and overlook the 80 percent of the time that you fail. You have to remember that baseball players who fail 70 percent of the time (and are successful 30 percent of the time) are often considered the best in the league. Some insight into the guiding principles of successful people that I have worked with can be seen though things that they do:

1. They commit to a dream.
2. They translate their dreams into daily goals.
3. They never forget their priorities: God, Family, and Career.
4. They see failures as learning opportunities.
5. They never quit.

The first and most important requirement is to commit to a dream. Everyone has dreams, but not everyone is willing to commit to that dream. Those who want to become physicians realize that there is a clear path to becoming a physician. First, they have to make the grades in high school in order to get into an acceptable university. Then they have to make the grades that will allow them to be considered for medical school. In addition to that, they have to prepare for the entrance examinations for medical school. If they commit to the dream and each critical step along the way, they will ultimately be admitted to medical school. Nothing, absolutely nothing, in life is either free or accidental. Success is a choice, and it begins with your willingness to commit to your own life's dream.

The second thing that "I can!" people do is to translate their dreams into daily goals. A friend once told me the story about how he taught new salespeople. He asked them to set their career goals, then he worked with them to figure out just how many people they needed to call on each day in order to meet their goals. Not surprisingly, the people who set and met their daily contact goals were successful. Those who did not meet their daily goals were not successful in the long run. To succeed, you must translate your dreams into daily goals, it's just that simple.

The third thing that "I can!" people do is to commit to balance in their lives. That is what Mary Kay taught me; God first, family second, and work third is extremely important. I've known a lot of people who thought that money and success would make them happy only to wake up one day and realize that they had sacrificed their faith or their family on the alter of success. I believe that the only time success is meaningful is when we have balanced lives. Anything else is hollow.

The fourth characteristic of successful people is that they see failure as a learning opportunity. The "I can't!" person will say: "See, I told you so. I do not have the talent to be successful." Conversely, the "I can!" person will evaluate each failure and use that as an opportunity to improve.

Finally, there is the idea of persistence. Quitters never win and winners never quit! History is filled with stories of people who have spent much of their lives as failures, only to go on to become successful. How are they different than their less successful counterparts? It's simple: They don't quit.

Being in Business for Yourself

One of the things about the Mary Kay opportunity is that you are in business by yourself but you are not alone. The way you run your business is your call. You decide when to get up in the morning, you don't have anyone telling you what to do, your day and your life is all up to you. But there is another side to that coin. In most cases, people with careers in sales work independently. A commission-only sales career is unquestionably one of those careers in which you are alone and out on a limb.

Another aspect I enjoy about my career in direct sales is that there are a lot of other women out there that want exactly the same thing that I want. When I made the decision to stop pursuing a typical "day job" and go into business for myself, I was scared to death. At the same time, I knew that it was something that I had to do for my family and myself if I ever wanted to achieve my own personal American dream. When my son was younger, I had the ability to plan my day so that I could take him to school, pick him up, and be there for those special moments in his life. In fact, that was probably one of the most important aspects that led me to the Mary Kay opportunity. I wanted the freedom to keep my personal priorities . . . God, Family, Career, in that order. I have never once regretted "going out on the limb" so that I could have the freedom to call my own shots. All of the fruit is out on the limb . . . think about the apple tree. After all, isn't that what the American dream is all about?

There is one common characteristic about all people who sell, regardless of industry. When it comes to getting hired at most companies, people do not care about how many college degrees you have, all they really care about is whether or not you can sell. One thing that most people will tell you, there is really no typical salesperson. Every salesperson I have met has had their own unique background, education, personality, and style; the only consistent characteristic among successful salespeople is an "I can!" attitude. The good news is that an "I can!" attitude can be learned if you are willing to try.

Becoming an "I Can!" Person

One trend I have observed during my years with Mary Kay is that success breeds success. I often see women who would like to have their own business, but are convinced that they do not have the interpersonal skills or aggressiveness to sell. In working with people like that, I have found if I can get them to have just one little taste of success, they are usually on their way. People who want to become physicians do not just go out and enroll in medical school. They usually start with one college course so they can get a feel for how they like the field.

When it comes to selling, I am one of the most fortunate people I know. I have a product that almost sells itself, so if I can figure out some way to get that product into someone's hands, I usually make a sale. I think that is what is so exciting to those that I introduce to the Mary Kay opportunity. It's all about getting the product into the hands of the customer . . . then the product sells itself. People like a good product.

It's not too difficult to ask someone to come to have a complimentary facial. More often than not, the people who come to get a free facial will be like a lot of those who have pursued their Mary Kay business for many years: The product is what gets their attention. That is why I feel that I am so fortunate to be in the business I am in. I get to invite people to do something that benefits them and makes them feel better about themselves. In a lot of ways, my career is not selling; it is helping others. I get very inspired when I think about the role I play in people's lives.

In my business, success breeds success. People don't really mind extending friendships to offer a complimentary facial. Once someone sees how absolutely enjoyable and easy it is to be a part of the Mary Kay opportunity, they often want to know how they can become a part of it.

One Step at a Time

Lenora Anderson is one of those people who has taken one step at a time and done well for many years in her business. Lenora was introduced to Mary Kay by her sister, Dee Denison. Lenora had spent many years working as an executive secretary, and really did not have much interest in becoming involved in sales. More than that, Lenora did not think she had the ability to be much of a salesperson. Lenora's sister Dee took her under her wing and taught her how to become one of those "I can!" people . . . one step at a time.

The first thing Dee did was to get Lenora to commit to inviting her friends to three meetings where they would receive complimentary facials. Although she was still not convinced, Lenora did it anyway. Dee was to conduct the meetings as a way to teach Lenora the process. That first week went pretty well, and all of a sudden, Lenora was excited.

Lenora has spent much of her time over the years in building a fairly large base of customers. In the beginning, she was only one of four people in the Kansas City area who sold Mary Kay products. After selling Mary Kay products for a while, she decided that she really liked it a lot. She liked it so much, in fact, that she decided she could earn more selling Mary Kay products than she could in her job as an executive secretary. As Lenora says, "I have never regretted my decision to become a Beauty Consultant or a Sales Director, and still to this day I continue to thank Dee for not giving up on me. I have built a great customer base, and am still selling to some of my first customers from over 30 years ago."

One of the Sales Directors who lives in the Kansas City area along with Lenora is Winnie Thorp-Rapp. I met Winnie just after I had begun my Mary Kay business and from the beginning, we had a great relationship.

Winnie never really worked in the business world. She had married, moved to Colorado, and had five children. Her life as a mother had taken up most of her time.

During her time in a little town in Colorado, Winnie began thinking about going to work. It was not that she wanted to go to work, she really wanted to stay at home and care for her children. The problem was, her husband was an alcoholic and was becoming increasingly abusive. She knew that because of his alcoholism she would need to be able to provide for her children one day soon. She also realized that the nearest job to her home was probably at least an hour and a half drive from the little town in which she lived. That was when Winnie discovered the Mary Kay opportunity.

After Winnie committed to her Mary Kay business, it was not long before her husband decided that they needed to move to Arizona. Things had not changed much at home, but Winnie had become even more committed to being able to provide her children with some options. Winnie had four children from her first marriage and a daughter from her second. She had become more and more concerned about the affects of her husband's alcoholism on her children.

Once in Arizona, Winnie says that she really discovered what it meant to be a part of the Mary Kay family. She also realized that you can "take your business with you." "What I found," says Winnie, "was a group of supportive, caring women who were willing to do just about anything to help me succeed. I cannot tell you what that meant to me to have such a caring group of women around me during my time of need."

A few years later, Winnie's marriage finally ended. Winnie returned to the Kansas City area and resumed her Mary Kay business. That's when I had the privilege of meeting her. During the next 10 years, Winnie continued to pursue her business and care for the remaining child in her household, her daughter. Winnie believes that her business really made a difference in her life and the lives of her children. "When I look back, I can see that my commitment to pursue my business while being there for my children had a powerful impact on their lives. I am so thankful that I was given the opportunity to do that," said Winnie.

When it comes to her Mary Kay business, Winnie often downplays her successes by comparing herself to some of her more financially successful counterparts. I think that her children would disagree with that. Winnie found a way to be there for her children during a time that was filled with difficulty at home.

I Can!

Making the commitment to "I can!" is often not about making hundreds of thousands of dollars or getting recognition. "I can!" is all about recognizing God's provision for you, or believing in yourself, or taking care of family. The first step is walking through that door of opportunity. That first small step provides the most meaningful opportunities in life.

I challenge you to think about what you want your life to be about. Your dreams might have to do with family, or providing for someone you love. I want to tell you one thing today: You Can! Now is the time to take charge of your life and your future.

Chapter 8

Think Positive . . . Live Positive

One characteristic shared by many people I meet is that they often start their days, and live their lives, with a negative attitude.

Researchers conducted a study of patients who were given comedy movies to watch while they were in the hospital. The medical professionals were astounded to discover that laughter seemed to alleviate pain and promote healing in a majority of the patients. Many of those same patients had not made any progress toward healing prior to the experiment with the movies.

I think it is time to ask a question: Did all the women whose stories I've presented in this book and who overcame their fears and feelings of inadequacy, have an innate ability to be successful? Of course they did. That is my point. You are no different. You have a sleeping giant inside of you, but to comprehend just how capable you are takes learning how to think positively.

It's about Discovering You

There are some schools of thought that believe that by "visualizing" an event, you can make it happen. While I do not believe that is an accurate account of how the human mind works, I once heard a story about a high school basketball team who imagined themselves winning. Two weeks before playoffs, their coach told the entire team to sit in the gym and literally "see" themselves shooting perfect shots for 30 minutes every day. There actually was an improvement in how the team played after that. The movie *Hoosiers* is about such a team and a coach who taught the team to believe in themselves.

It is important to get past negative and distorted ideas and see yourself and your actions in positive ways. If you have not been able to achieve your potential, it is probably because you have been telling yourself things that are untrue. To break through our inaccurate beliefs, we may need to unlearn lessons we learned about ourselves in childhood.

Before you make that next sales call, picture yourself making the perfect call. Such thinking has a positive impact on behavior and decisions. Like the basketball team, when you focus your thinking on doing something well, it is easier to follow through and do it well in real life.

As I think back to my childhood, growing up with an alcoholic father was challenging. After my father died, my self-esteem took a lot of hits from the children around me. Many people who had been cordial and friendly turned their backs on us once it became apparent that my family had no money left. As a result of much taunting and rejection, I grew up with some serious misconceptions about myself.

There were still a few people in my life who worked really hard to help me develop a positive attitude about myself. My mother was probably the most influential person in that area of my life. Regardless of all my mother's encouragement, when I arrived in America, I was not sure that I had the skills and talent to succeed. However, as I developed friendships, many people helped me discover that I was much more capable than I once thought.

My sister Donna helped me make one of my most important breakthroughs. After telling her about the wonderful Mary Kay opportunity, she challenged me to tell others. She talked about the wonderful opportunity that I had, and how important it was for me to share that with others. That discussion, helped me develop a powerful, positive attitude. In some ways, I had been allowing my old insecurities to rule my life. It was then that I decided that I had the ability, and I was committed to do it.

Another advantage to having a positive attitude is that the people around you notice it. People can sense a person's attitude, and in many ways that attitude reflects on the product being sold. There is a saying, "people don't buy products, they buy people." I have thought a lot about that concept, and I believe it is true. If you are a positive person who exudes confidence, others will trust you. Customers look forward to hearing from you.

But there is more to it than that. Individuals are continuously involved in communicating on various levels. Thus, a positive attitude communicates itself in a subconscious way. There are people whom you meet and instantly trust without really knowing why. Feeling that you can trust an individual results from unspoken communication that the person radiates. Ultimately, having a positive attitude can go straight to the bottom line. I often tell people at sales events: "Your attitude will determine your altitude in life; and in a lot of ways, your bank account really reflects your attitude."

Don't Send Me

I first met Trish Reuser at the Mary Kay's annual Seminar in Dallas in 1992. Trish is a person I admire. She is always winning awards for excellence in sales. However, Trish did not start out that way.

While studying the Old Testament prophet, Moses, Trish found herself identifying with the fear and insecurity Moses felt when faced with the task of delivering the Israelites out of Egypt. Trish believes this story of overcoming one's insecurities is similar to the challenges she's faced in her own life. "That was me," says Trish. "Just like

Moses had, I wanted to raise my hand and say: 'God, please do not send me. I am slow of speech and not eloquent." Trish recalls that just as Moses took that first step and trusted God, she too decided to trust that she had the ability to achieve what she set out to do.

When she began her business, Trish was a Navy wife living in Virginia. Faced with her husband's immanent separation from the Navy, she began to think about what she would do once he was no longer traveling and away from home. Trish decided that she would like to pursue a career now that they would not be so transient.

Trish was invited to attend a class where she could try out the Mary Kay products. "At the time, I did not even wash my face at night, so I had little interest in cosmetics," Trish told me. But after she had her first facial, she saw an immediate difference in her complexion. A few days later, the host called her and told her that she thought she would be great at selling Mary Kay products. "I could not imagine myself selling anything," said Trish. Even though Trish felt that she was not a strong communicator and definitely not sales consultant material, her friend was certain she would be great at selling, and that was what finally convinced her to give it a try.

When Trish first began selling products, she did not have any plans of becoming a Sales Director. Since Sales Directors are frequently required to speak to large audiences, Trish had no intentions of reaching that level in the organization. Not seeing herself as being an effective public speaker, she was content working as an Independent Sales Consultant. A few years after starting her Mary Kay business, Trish recognized that her area was in need of a Sales Director, so she tried to encourage a number of her Consultants to give it a try. One by one, her Consultants replied that Trish was the best candidate and encouraged her to become the Sales Director instead. Despite her apprehension, Trish decided to make the commitment and became a Sales Director.

Trish has gone on to have a wonderful business. Trish earned the use of four career cars early in her career. Again, because of the encouragement of her team, she decided to try to qualify for a pink Cadillac. She just earned the use of her tenth Cadillac. That's quite an accomplishment for someone who did not think that she had the ability to sell.

The thread running through Trish's successful sales business is the positive reinforcement she received from those around her. There were many times that Trish felt inadequate or even totally lacking in the talent area. In every case, someone came along and convinced Trish to change her thinking from negative to positive. You have to think positive if you are to accomplish positive things!

Think in Terms of Positive Possibilities

I have a friend who teaches people how to sail. He explained to me one of the discoveries he had made about how people learn. While teaching a group of beginners how to sail, he asked them to close their eyes and picture a sailboat slicing through the water. He asked them to watch how the boat tilted to the right or to the left and what the sails looked like as they pulled the boat forward. What he learned changed the way he taught people to sail.

As with learning anything you are unfamiliar with, one of the challenges of teaching people to sail is getting people to understand the mechanics behind the process. Much to my friend's amazement, once his students got a mental picture of how the sails would look when the boat would pivot right or left, they suddenly began sailing much better. He learned that once his students had a mental picture of what the sails should look like, they almost immediately set the boat's sails correctly.

That is what you have to do in learning how to be a successful salesperson. This is all about approaching your sales opportunity in a positive manner.

The first step in this process involves finding three people who will let you watch them work. Tell them you just want to observe them and their techniques. Watch them as they begin the sales process (telephone calls, etc.), and go on at least three appointments with each one. Here are some questions to think about:

> In calling the customer to get an appointment: What did each salesperson do as she approached the customer to get the appointment? Was she smiling while she was talking with the customer? Did you know you

can "hear" a smile on the phone? Could you pick up a positive attitude from the salesperson as she made the call and talked with the prospective customer?

During the sales call, watch for the three S's: Smile; Sense; Straight. First, did she start her contact with the customer with a *smile*? How did the customer respond? Second, as the appointment progressed, did the salesperson effectively *sense* what the customer was thinking and what her real needs were? Third, once she understood what the customer wanted, did she go *straight* to the customer's needs?

People show their feelings through their facial expressions. If they walk into a room with a frown on their face, people inevitably ask, "Are you okay?" No matter the kind of a day you might have had, you have to begin your relationship with your contacts in a positive way. People are attracted to others who smile; it's just that simple.

The second thing to observe is the various ways the customers respond to the salespeople. What does it mean when someone looks down while listening to a sales presentation? What does it mean when the person taps her feet or drums her fingers on a table? Observe the customers' faces when the salespeople smile at them. By the end of the presentations, you should be able to make a mental list of the different messages that the customers were sending to the salespeople . . . both positive and negative.

Another thing to watch for is whether or not the techniques used by the salespeople went straight to fulfilling the customers' needs. Some of the smartest sales professionals I know will often stop selling early in a sales presentation. Why do you think that happens?

First, experienced salespeople are perceptive enough to gain a clear understanding of what the customer is thinking. They can distinguish between false and genuine responses to buying opportunities. A false response might sound something like this: "I've just never had an interest in cosmetics." Notice that the customer is not really saying no, she is just trying to end the sales call. Another response might be, "My sister sells brand Z cosmetics. I would never be able to keep peace in the family if I didn't use brand Z." Notice that any challenge to the second customer would be unwise. It's a family issue. At the same time, look at the great opening you might have with the first customer (assuming you are selling cosmetics) by simply offering them a complimentary facial. It's important to remember that negative responses are usually not the true feeling of the customer. Sometimes, a negative response may simply mean that it is not the right time to discuss the issue, or maybe they have had a bad day. All of those situations give you an opportunity to be a considerate and effective salesperson.

Self-Fulfilling Prophecy

Remembering daily to "think positive—live positive" can be a powerful force in your life. When you begin to approach every aspect of your life with that attitude, circumstances in your life begin to change. More importantly, you begin to change. You are not changing your circumstances—those may be out of your control. You are just changing your habits. If your habits become success oriented then you become a habitually successful person. Doesn't that sound wonderful?

Making a Positive Change

I want to tell you about Joni Pritchard—one of the fabulous people I have met along the way. Joni was already a success in her own right when she discovered the Mary Kay opportunity. In 1988, Joni began selling Mary Kay products while she continued her job as a full-time sales professional with an ad agency. She sold television advertising and was doing well in her commission-only job.

One day in March 1992, the head of the agency asked to meet with Joni. It seems that one of the other salespeople in the agency had been playing golf with clients from two of Joni's accounts. After a short conversation, the head of the agency informed Joni that she needed to give up those accounts since the other salesman had built a relationship with her clients.

At that time, Joni had been dabbling in her Mary Kay business. She managed to have a few appointments with customers each week, but had never really been too serious about it due to the success she was having in her full-time job. Joni went home that night and began thinking about what had happened at work that day. The more she thought about it, the more convinced she was that she was tired of working for others, especially the boss who had just let another salesperson poach two accounts she had spent a great deal of time on. The next day Joni resigned her position at the ad agency. She made the commitment to be successful in her Mary Kay business.

In August 1992, Joni earned the use of her first career car. In January 1993, she qualified to become a Sales Director. Her second daughter was born in 1995, and Joni was able to be home to care for both of her children because of the freedom her work provided. In 2001, her marriage ended in divorce.

Because of the divorce, Joni was distraught. As she thought about her circumstances and all of the challenges she faced as a single mom, she initially felt that the rest of her life would be a struggle. Joni then began to think about all of the things she wanted to achieve, and instead decided to focus on that. One of the first goals on her list was losing weight. She began disciplining herself and as a result she slowly started to lose weight. She also decided that she was going to begin training to run a marathon. She credits her mentors at Mary Kay with a lot of the design for her training program. These women taught her to think positive and to set goals. But that is not the end of the story.

Joni lost over 100 pounds due to her training regime for running a marathon. She went on to run in the Honolulu Marathon. Joni's positive attitude about her life carried her through the grueling months of preparation for that race, and her positive attitude drove her to finish the 26.2 miles marathon:

> "Wow! What a thrill to finish that race and cross the finish line. My Mary Kay experience taught me how to focus, set goals, and reach them. I am grateful to some fabulous mentors . . .
>
> In 2002, I designed and had my own home built. I found the property and hired the contractor—all with my Mary Kay commissions. Happily, in 2004 I married Jim Augsburger, a very sweet gentleman whom I met at a potluck dinner at a Christian Social Club."

Joni figured out that living life with a positive attitude is a lot more enjoyable, not to mention financially rewarding. I have been so pleased to watch Joni as she "positively" went from discouragement to success. She is an inspiration.

Think Positive—Live Positive

I want to close this chapter with the thought I began with. I also want to put sales aside for a moment and talk about life. In sales, success is a choice. The same is true for happiness. You can choose to live life as a victim or you can choose to live as a victor. In focusing on the most important parts of our lives, God first, family second, and work third, I challenge you today to make the commitment to focus on the positives of every aspect of your life.

Chapter 9

Turn Defeat into Success

It seems that the worst of all circumstances are often the launching pad for people's greatest successes. When we look at the top salesperson or the Olympic athlete, we often fail to notice where they started and what it took for them to get to the top. More often than not, they started at the bottom. Is it possible that defeat or adversity is the origin of success?

Chuck Swindoll, the inspirational pastor and author, tells of the humble beginnings of some very prominent people. Walt Disney was fired by a newspaper editor for "lack of ideas." Henry Ford declared bankruptcy twice before finally becoming a successful automobile manufacturer. General George Patton, President Woodrow Wilson, Albert Einstein, Leonardo da Vinci, and Prime

Minister Winston Churchill all entered this world with learning disabilities.[1]

Sometimes we learn life's most important lessons simply by watching others go through hardship. When I look back at my early life in Ireland and how my father died leaving us almost penniless, and how my mother struggled just to get by, I realize how discouraging life's early challenges can be. When I think about how I ended up coming to America to discover unlimited opportunity, I also look back and remember how my mother always told me to forget about the circumstances beyond my control and focus on the abilities that God had given me. Disabled with the birth of her first child, and abandoned by my father, my mother never lost her desire to achieve the very best.

Defeat Is Often How God Talks with You

Recall some of the lowest times in your life. Have you ever failed so miserably that you felt that you just could not face your friends or your family? Those are the times God talks with us. I believe He speaks to us through our circumstances.

What is so powerful about defeat that it can transform our lives? Defeat and hardship, whether they are a result of our actions or not, teach lessons about life. Ultimately,

[1] Chuck Swindoll, "From the Heart," *Kindred Spirit*, vol. 22, no. 3 (1998), Dallas Theological Seminary.

failure can be our best teacher. For example, if my interactions with others constantly end in arguments, I am failing in my communication. As a logical as well as an emotional person, at some point I must acknowledge that I am responsible for those relationship issues. My role is to figure out what I am doing to continually encounter these types of problems.

The same is true for sales. If I talk with 10 different people on the phone trying to set up appointments and I fail with all 10, I must be doing something wrong. Since only I can change myself, I must start there. Acknowledging that you are responsible for the outcome of sales calls, and most other things in life, while discouraging at first, can ultimately be empowering. Although you may be falling short of achieving a goal, it is within your power to change the results.

This is an important point to keep in mind: Successful people are not victims. The world is filled with people who want you to believe that you are a victim. Believing that you are at a disadvantage can actually put you at a disadvantage. I categorically reject the idea that circumstances in our lives dictate the outcome. I refuse to be a victim. I am a child of an alcoholic father but I refuse to allow that to control my life. I was not raised with all the advantages of wealth and opportunity that many around me had. I refused to allow that to control my life.

Defeat or hardship in life is never permanent. They are bumps in the road of life and you have to make a choice about how you are going to deal with them. If you let them drive you off your course, you are simply accepting that you are a victim, and that your course is beyond your control. If you look back with joy at how you dealt with those bumps in the road—and overcame them—you are on your way to becoming a successful person. Every obstacle is an opportunity in disguise.

Learning Your Way to Success

Most people find it difficult to hear criticism. However, in order to grow we must learn to accept criticism and use it to improve ourselves. Criticisms as well as failure are simply a means to achieving excellence. I often find training new salespeople is like walking a tight rope. An honest and frank evaluation of her performance may discourage the new person and, in the process, convince her that she has no potential. An overly lenient review where observations are sugar coated will prevent that person from recognizing the reasons for her failures and rectifying them. The challenge is balancing your input so that you help the person improve her skills without discouraging her.

Teaching others is the most enjoyable aspect of my business and it is often why I get out of bed in the morning. I absolutely soar when one of the Consultants on my team is successful. Further, there is nothing more exciting than seeing someone you taught learn to overcome defeat with success.

Soaring from Defeat to Victory

One of the Consultants I have had the honor of being associated with is Ruthie Bresette-Mount. Ruthie is one of those people who grew up under difficult circumstances, but achieved success regardless of that fact. Ruthie spent the first nine years of her life living in a 700-square-foot apartment with her six siblings. She told me about how her parents would often hide a few dollars around the apartment, just in case there were unexpected expenses.

Ruthie is one of those people who does not allow her circumstances to determine her fate. After graduating from high school, Ruthie began working in retail sales. She worked and went to college part time for a number of years. Finally, eight or so years later, Ruthie graduated with her bachelor's degree and was ready to go out and conquer the world. With her new degree in hand, she began applying for entry-level positions within large companies. Ruthie never found a corporate job, but instead, continued to work in retail.

By the time she reached her thirties, Ruthie was still single and still working long hours in retail. But Ruthie was not ready to be defined by this set of circumstances. A friend of Ruthie's had tried for over three years to get her to attend a Mary Kay function and finally she succeeded. It did not take long for Ruthie to decide to give the opportunity a try. That was in 1987.

Ruthie still needed to work her retail job for 40 to 60 hours a week to make the money she needed. She began to do fairly well selling Mary Kay products, but still needed to keep her retail job part time to make ends meet. When she turned 35 years old, Ruthie started on a professional as well as a spiritual journey in her life. In some ways, she was beginning to feel like a failure. In contemplating her professional life, she felt that until now she had been giving her Mary Kay business a half-hearted effort. In her personal life, she wanted to find someone she could share her life with.

In Ruthie's words, "God began working on me." What Ruthie realized was that she did not have the right attitude for success. She had an attitude that was more about getting by than getting to the top. That applied to her business life as well as her personal life. That was when she made the conscious decision to give her business her all. With a renewed faith, she set out to achieve her dreams.

As I was thinking about Ruthie's story, I was reminded of a favorite scripture verse:

> Blessed be the God and Father of our Lord Jesus Christ, who has blessed us with every spiritual blessing in the heavenly places in Christ . . .
>
> Ephesians 1:3 (New American Standard Version)

Just as God's blessing is always there, Ruthie's ability to succeed was always there. The key is to make the decision to go from discouragement to direction. That is what Ruthie did.

Ruthie's life and her business took off at that point. Not only was her faith ignited, so was her business. After 10 years, Ruthie quit her job and devoted herself to her Mary Kay business full time.

When Ruthie made the decision to go from defeat to victory, her life began to change. Today, Ruthie's life is drastically different. She has earned the use of company cars for quite a while, has progressed up the career path to become a Senior Sales Director, and has designed and built her own 4,000-square-foot home. That's a long way from the small apartment she grew up in with her six siblings. But Ruthie is not going to live in that new house alone either; she got married three years ago. The best way to conclude Ruthie's story is to let you read just a few words from an e-mail she wrote to me. I think you will see exactly what happened in Ruthie's life . . . and what can happen in yours.

"I knew that 'I' had to change before my situation would change! I began to pray often and learned how to have a true relationship with the Lord. I listened to Christian talk radio and Mary Kay educational and inspirational tapes over and over and over! You see, the top Mary Kay Sales Directors thought differently than I did, and I realized that while listening to them! My thoughts also changed when I occupied them with the Lord's word! Those two things totally transformed my life. Then, and only then, was I able and ready to move forward with my business. Praise the Lord!

"That next year I took my unit to our first unit circle of $300,000 and my belief barriers were broken! I became very excited for the Lord to use me however He wanted and I totally believed that my Mary Kay business was His vehicle to do so! You see, we all want to follow a leader, and once I became one, I was able to take others along with me! What a fulfilling way to live each and every day! He also provided my perfect, handsome, loving husband three years ago!"

Ruthie is an inspiration to me and to others around her as well. Ruthie told me that her next step is to achieve Independant Sales Director status by 2006. I have no doubt that she will make it.

How to Turn Defeat into Success

As I consider my own life, I realize that I could have stayed in Ireland, gotten married, and spent the rest of my life near my family. In many ways that would have been a wonderful life to have, but I felt that there was more that I wanted to achieve in my life. When I came to America, I began to live my own "American dream." One of the fascinating things I have noticed about my American dream is that it has had a powerful effect on my family as well. My sister, Donna, is enjoying success in her Mary Kay business. My mom has her own savings account so she can buy herself special things, travel around the world, and more than that, she can come to visit us often.

When I arrived in the United States that first time, I experienced a lot of defeat and hardship in my eighteen years. Our family struggled financially, and we were no longer accepted as members of the community in which we had lived. As I think about it today, I cannot imagine coming to a new country with only $20 in my pocket in order to take a job that paid me $20 a week. But that is how I turned defeat into victory.

I have found that there are five characteristics that I commonly see in people who are able to turn defeat into victory.

1. *Trust in God.* When I think about Ruthie's life, it is clear that she reached a point in her life at which she turned her life over to God. While everyone has his or her own belief system, it is important to have faith. I believe that God is a loving God. God is real. He can change lives. I believe that a successful life begins with faith in the God who created you. Mary Kay Ash believed that as well.
2. *Dream big dreams.* If your dreams and goals in life are mediocre, mediocrity is exactly what you will achieve. You will be successful in fulfilling that dream. I encourage you to think more in terms of possibilities than limitations. The main reason most people never discover all of their potential and abilities is because they accept opinions about themselves that are not true. I challenge you to sit down and write your big dreams on a piece of paper. You will be

astounded by the impact that the simple act of writing your dreams down will have on your thinking. In some ways, the dreams you dream have an impact on the dreams you get to live.

3. *Develop a plan.* When you read about the lives of some of the most successful people in history, you find that many of them have one thing in common: They all failed at some point. We all fail, so what is the difference between someone who fails and gives up on life, and someone who fails and uses that experience as a launching pad for unbelievable success? The answer to that question is that the second type of person develops a plan. Mary Kay used to tell us "we fail forward to success."

   Once you hit bottom, the only direction you can go is up. The only way you get out is with a plan. A plan is what guides our efforts. More importantly, as we develop our plan we are developing an awareness of each step that we must take in order to achieve success.

4. *Create small successes.* It was Confucius who said, "A journey of a thousand miles begins with a single step." In the case of success, it begins with creating just one event of success. It may be a phone call to a prospective client. It may be your first sale. Someone once said to me "Inspiration begins with pushing your chair up to the desk." That was their way of saying that in order to be successful, you have to have a beginning. That is especially true of success.

The only way that we can begin being successful is to begin. You must have a plan to achieve that success.

Sales are a tough business and it is often filled with failure. As I have said before, there is always a basis from which you can plan your success. If you know that you have to call 10 people every day to get one new customer, you have to focus on success related to making those 10 calls. You have to rejoice when you accomplish that task. The good news is, if you made those 10 calls, you have that new customer. So, one success creates another. I encourage you to think about how many ways you can be successful every day, then go for it!

5. *Persevere.* The only difference between winners and losers is that winners don't quit. If you have a desire to be successful in whatever you want to do, you have to be one of those people who persevere.

   Many of the people who enter sales quit. Let's consider why they quit. Do you think it's because they do not have the talent or ability to sell? I do not believe this is so. They quit because they are not committed to becoming something different. The individuals who quit are often more comfortable feeling like a victim than taking charge of their own success.

Success Is a Choice

It is ultimately your choice to be successful. If you want to climb a tall mountain, you will become discouraged if all you look at is the highest peak. Success, however, is right there in front of you. It may be the first little hill, or a goal on the way up. But the bottom line is simply that it is your choice.

Defeat is often the defining moment in peoples' lives. In some cases, they decide that they will never be able to overcome the embarrassment or the devastation of that defeat. In the case of others, they consider defeat to be a stepping stone on the way to being successful. Defeat only serves to define where they are, not where they will end up.

Which one will you decide to be? I suspect that you have dreams, or at least had dreams. You must reconsider the way you perceive and respond to the defeats in your life and begin to look at them as defining the past and not the future. It really is your choice.

Chapter 10

Integrity

The single most important attribute you must possess to ensure consistent and continued success in a sales career is integrity. While some might say that is a fairly obvious statement, there is much more to having integrity than just saying you do. Adhering to some moral or ethical code in sales is essential to developing and maintaining good customer relations.

A lack of integrity can destroy personal as well as business relationships forever and can quickly convince someone not to do business with you again. In fact, as a consumer, haven't you had exactly that experience yourself? I have personally seen salespeople pressure customers into making decisions just so they can fulfill their quotas. This type of behavior fails to consider the needs of the customer.

Who Are You?

Ethics are at the foundation of every relationship in a sales career. If you intentionally mislead others just to make a sale, you will not be successful in a sales career. Without integrity, there can be no relationship, and without developing relationships, you cannot establish a customer base.

One of the things I have observed about salespeople is that they usually live their lives in the same way that they sell. If they are honest in their personal lives, they are the same in their selling relationships. It's as simple as this: Who are you?

One thing a lot of people fail to notice is the positive impact that personal integrity has on sales. Once customers discover that you are a person of integrity, they begin viewing you as a consultant rather than as a salesperson. Customers will invite your opinion because they trust that you have their best interests in mind. In the end, you are not only selling a product; you are selling you. It is extremely difficult to take a customer away from an honest salesperson. When your customers discover they are working with an honest person, they will have no interest in dealing with other salespeople. They will have found what they want: Someone they can trust to put their interests first. That is the basis for successful business relationships.

Beware of Sales "Methods"

If you have been working in sales for a while, or if you are just entering the profession, I want to caution you. Many sales professionals conduct sales seminars that teach salespeople to avoid discussing competitors' product advantages, focusing the customer's interest on the positive attributes of your products. There are many ways to do this, but I believe that all of them are wrong. Using this method, you never really answer the customer's question. Basically what happens when a salesperson uses that approach is that she ignores the customer's concerns and questions. By treating an issue superficially, the salesperson hopes to avoid dealing with the issue. We all know that a percentage of the buyers will allow you to steamroll over them just because they are intimidated or unwilling to disagree with you. In many cases, they will go ahead and buy from you. There is one thing to remember: That will most likely be the last time they buy from you.

How to Destroy a Relationship

In the past few years, people in the business world have been taught a number of unforgettable lessons. Those lessons, while not learned first-hand, apply to us as sales professionals just as they apply to the people who made ethical missteps—who lacked integrity.

When you talk about companies that employ dishonest, deceitful, and fraudulent tactics, the company many of us think of is Enron. As the facts of the case unfolded, it became apparent that the people involved failed to operate from a position of integrity. While it is possible to occasionally do something dishonest and temporarily cover it up, in almost every case such actions ultimately are exposed.

Integrity is a character trait that describes who you are, but having integrity is a goal we must continually strive toward. Watching the media coverage of the Enron scandal, it is apparent that had a few people with integrity taken a stand against the deceptive accounting practices, Enron might still be a thriving, growing company. The company had employed some of the brightest people around. The problem was, "who they were" was not acceptable.

Another player in the Enron scandal was Arthur Andersen and Company—one of the world's most respected accounting firms for many years. Yet, all it took was one fraudulent act, and Andersen is no longer. Think about the extent of damage that just one dishonest act can cause. While most of the employees at Andersen conducted business in an ethical manner, one isolated group of people decided to act dishonestly. I would like to point out that in the case of the Enron incident one senior executive did step forward and try to deal with the dishonesty. Although the actions of the individual did not prevent the problems, it is possible that the same actions at another company might prevent a similar outcome. In much the same way, all it takes is one dishonest act to destroy your personal reputation.

Although it is now apparent that a number of Andersen employees had an opportunity to stop the dishonest practices, not one took action. Had someone in charge of the Enron account taken a stand for integrity, that situation might never have happened. In both these instances, we see that integrity is critical in success and in life. To the public that witnessed these events, their assessment of who these companies are will probably never be repaired. Andersen is gone and Enron declared bankruptcy. Dishonesty in some ways becomes a life sentence, because in many cases "who you are" to outsiders is defined by a single event.

Two Keys to Integrity

Those involved in sales may have encountered sales consultants who padded the numbers just a little. It might have been for the purpose of winning a sales contest or fulfilling a quota, but it often happens at some point in a sales career. There are two principles that will help you maintain integrity.

First, the founder of Mary Kay Inc., Mary Kay Ash based her company on the Golden Rule: "Do unto others as you would have them do unto you." From the inception of her business, she made sure that every person whether they be employees or independent contractors like myself understood that was the way she wanted to do business. Mary Kay wanted every member of her team to understand that they would be treated according to the Golden Rule. She also wanted them to understand that they were to treat their customers in the same way.

I had the opportunity to observe Mary Kay and her career from 1986 until she passed away almost 16 years later. In addition to the basic integrity that was the foundation of her life, Mary Kay considered the potential impact of the decisions she made on the lives of others before making a decision that would negatively impact the people within her company or the customers loyal to her. Mary Kay believed that you must put people before profits. According to her philosophy, if you live the Golden Rule, the profits will follow.

Over the years, Mary Kay was featured on national television and in magazines, and she was the recipient of numerous awards. Looking at her financial accomplishments, it's easy to forget the magnitude of her personal accomplishments. She was someone who exuded integrity. When it came to providing for her employees, she never asked how much benefits or incentives would cost. When she saw there was a need, she responded. When confronted with decisions, she consistently opted to take the position of unquestioned integrity and always wanted to "seek the best for others."

Another key to maintaining your personal integrity is to remain above reproach. This entails avoiding even the appearance of impropriety. The reality of business and of life is that it only takes one black mark on your integrity for your career to be finished.

Living a life that is above reproach is an excellent way to avoid negative situations. One common practice among salespeople involves soliciting customers to place large orders a bit early, so that salespeople can reach a quota or win a contest. Even though the salespeople may have a close personal relationship with the customer that is not a situation in which they are above reproach.

Such behavior does not pass the "sleep test." If you do something and you find that you have trouble going to sleep that night because you are worrying about what you did, you probably did not do the right thing. No career is worth sacrificing for a momentary gain.

My father-in-law John and I had many talks when I was getting to know him. He was a firefighter in the Kansas City, Missouri, Fire Department and was hoping to one day be captain. Finally, a position opened up and John decided to go through the application process. He was exhilarated to find out that he was a contender for the position. He received a phone call from the Fire Chief telling him that he had been appointed to the Captain's position. John asked about his coworkers who he knew were higher on the list of candidates than he was. He was informed that because the department needed a minority in that position, they had skipped over the others on the list to pick him.

John was appalled. He felt that accepting the position was the wrong thing to do. He replied, "I will take the position when I earn it and not before." That day, John taught a lesson of integrity to his fellow workers and to his family. A man of integrity can sleep at night knowing that his actions and decisions are above reproach.

Just a Little White Lie

Many salespeople are tempted to tell what they consider "little white lies" to persuade customers to purchase what they are selling. I heard about a business broker who would call potential buyers and inform them that there was someone else looking at the businesses in which they were interested. He found that would often spur buyers to go ahead and make the decision to buy the businesses.

I have heard salespeople say similar things to get me to buy something. Remember the car salesman in an earlier chapter? He and his coworker played the part of a manager to put pressure on me to buy the car from him right then, undoubtedly to help him meet his quota. The last time I checked, a lie, even if it is not meant to injure or deceive is still a lie. Telling lies violates the basic principle at the foundation of all sales: The outcome has to be what is best for the customer.

The Glue That Lasts a Lifetime

Although people with many different personalities are successful in a sales business, the one commonality between all successful salespeople is that they have integrity. I've often said that there is no such thing as a *sales type.* While sales consultants who use deception sometimes achieve fantastic things in the short run, they ultimately lose customers. People prefer to do business with those who are ethical in their dealings.

If you want to attract and maintain customers, be sure that you are above reproach in everything you do. To do that, you may have to recommend a competitor's product. If it really is true that your competitor's product is what the customer needs, why should you even think about doing anything other than helping that customer buy the right product for herself?

You may lose a sale but inevitably you will gain a customer for life. Imagine what would happen to a car dealership that adopted that principle? I suspect that the customers would be swarming the place so they could do business with that dealership.

Integrity is the starting point for a sales career. It is the starting point for every sales transaction, and the foundation of sales success. As a customer or client, you do not really care how charming someone is as long as they are honest in their dealings with you. Success in sales is really all about "doing what is best for the customer." Integrity involves following through on that principle. You might call it the Golden Rule of Sales: Do what is best for the customer. Integrity is also a critical part of your relationship with God, your family, and your work. Integrity and success are inextricably linked together.

Chapter 11

Discover the Power of Your Dream

Before beginning this chapter, create a short list of goals that you have dreamed of reaching, but have never been able to achieve. Write out your list so that you can refer to them later.

What makes dreams so significant in our lives is that dreams are specific and exclusive to the individual. Dreams are as unique as the people who dream them. If everyone aspired to being CEOs of major companies, wouldn't life be boring? There are individuals who spend their entire lives working toward breeding the perfect dog and winning the Westminster Dog Show. Many men dream of winning a bass fishing tournament or playing a professional sport.

While men's dreams usually involve their individual accomplishments and success, women's dreams often involve other people. Whether they dream of being home to raise their children or having a successful career, women typically see themselves as part of a group. We want to help others and we want a good life for our families. Many women who succeed in their Mary Kay business initially pursued their career because they dreamed of being there for their families for all of the special moments, but they often found that they had to experience those moments second hand because they had to work.

The direct-selling industry provides opportunities for individuals to go into business for themselves. Rather than spending millions of dollars on marketing their products, direct-selling companies spend those dollars compensating their sales staff. It is not unusual for some corporations to spend over 50 percent of their revenue on advertising. Allocating these returns to salespeople instead is an effective way to market products. The benefits and incentives of a direct-selling career are what drive the diversity of people in direct selling. Many people see direct selling as a way of having their own business on the side and, in many cases, they never intend to quit their day jobs. One such person was Willois Smith.

When Willois was first invited to attend a Mary Kay meeting, she did not have any interest. Willois worked her way up from being a mainframe programmer to a lead programmer in her organization. Willois was content with her career, so she was not that interested in pursuing other opportunities. This is Willois' story of how she started her Mary Kay business:

> After being approached several times about purchasing the products, having a facial, attending a debut or whatever, I finally decided to accept an invitation to hear some people talk about the company. I had no idea what kind of affair I was about to attend, but I had, as Chuck Berry sang, "no particular place to go" that night so I thought it would fill the evening. I seem to recall this Sales Director (and my recruiter Debbie Battle) telling me about some hotshot sista that was going to speak. That sista was the fabulous Gloria Mayfield Banks, and Debbie seemed to adore her. So, I thought, why not attend.
>
> And I did. I heard several women tell their success stories, but I was most impressed when one of them said that she used to work in system operations and left her job to become a full-time consultant. Well, that must have been Gill. Being a former mainframe programmer and now a lead, I realized that this woman left a job that paid her a pretty good salary. So, there must be pretty good money in this business, huh?
>
> I recall another woman speaking of her long-term relationship with God. Even though she didn't say the words Jesus Christ or salvation, I was impressed that she even mentioned her faith. Hearing these two women's stories plus the fact that earning some extra money would have helped make ends meet inspired me to give it a try. I decided to sign my Independent Beauty Consultant Agreement thinking that I had a ready-made customer base.

Willois has received numerous awards for her sales success. She achieved that success working only a few hours a week for three years. Although her dream when she decided to become a Mary Kay Consultant was to earn an additional income, she has found that the friendships and opportunity have impacted her entire life. She has recruited over 20 new Consultants, including her two sons. Her dream now is to achieve Sales Director status at the same time as her sons and walk the stage at our annual seminar in Dallas with them beside her.

As Willois has grown and advanced in her business, she has made her dream of having a rewarding business come to fruition. It is rewarding for me to watch someone of her talent commit to growing her business even more. Dreams come in many different forms, but, regardless of the dream, achieving them has the power to change people's lives.

Dreams Crystallize Purpose

I had a friend whose college roommate, Carl, wanted to become a physician. Because premedical students must fulfill numerous biology requirements to complete their degrees, Carl inundated his life with anatomy information. He put drawings of the human circulatory system on the bottom of the upper bunk bed so that when he went to bed, the last thing he would see at night was that drawing. He put other drawings inside the medicine cabinet, so that he would see those as he opened the cabinet to shave in the morning. The drawings were everywhere.

Carl had a dream of becoming a doctor and realized that he had to be exceptional along the way. The drawings were a way of making sure that he focused on achieving his dream every day of his academic life. His dream was always before him. He had a dream to become a physician so he could help others. That dream was crystallized in his daily purpose.

One of the ways that Mary Kay's dream is crystallized in the Mary Kay organization is through the company's mission statement: "Enriching women's lives." I have witnessed dramatic changes in the lives of those who become Beauty Consultants. In some cases, their friends and families have never believed in them. In others, they needed a loving "push" from someone who wanted the very best for them in order to take the first steps in pursuing their business. Regardless, the one consistent comment that I hear from people who are associated with the independent salesforce is that their lives have been enriched by their new Mary Kay friends.

All of the women who have a Mary Kay business had dreams; it's just that at some point their dreams became their purpose. The philosophy God first, family second, work third describes how many people would like to live their lives if given the opportunity. The corporate rat race, however, is such that the priorities required to be successful today seem to put work first, work second, work third, and if you have a little time for God and your family that's okay, just don't miss any of your work!

Dreams Inspire Action

One of the big problems that most of us face is not related to whether or not we *have* dreams. It is related to getting past all of the excuses we use to justify why we are not pursuing our dreams. If you ask someone what her dreams are, she will undoubtedly have a dream that she has not yet achieved. If you then ask her why she has not pursued her dreams, she will invariably have a list of reasons.

Dreams can be so powerful that when we actually focus on them they become the basis for all of our actions. During the first few years of my business, I struggled to try to meet the goals I set for myself. I still had that same dream in my heart that compelled me to come to America, but all of the details of life, family, a demanding job, as well as a lack of action, kept me from moving forward.

My life only changed when I began to execute my dream. The change was dramatic. In a lot of ways, I had been allowing my circumstances to control my actions. When I began to focus on my dream, my dream began to drive my actions. In looking back, I was one of the fortunate ones. My husband, Vince, my family, and many of my friends encouraged me to work toward my dream. I was the one who was not yet willing to take action to achieve my dream. When your dream becomes the focus of your life, that is when you begin taking action toward achieving it.

For those who make the decision to begin their Mary Kay business, this is especially true. It is not unusual for a woman to spend 5 or 10 years casually working at building her personal business and do acceptably well. Then one day she wakes up and realizes that she has dreams and even though "acceptable" is comfortable, it is time for her to take charge of her life. When this happens, all of the other circumstances in her life begin to change.

If you are allowing your circumstances to control your destiny, you will never be able to reach your dream. Only when you act on your dream are you able to change your circumstances.

Take Action on Your Dream

It is your responsibility to take the first step toward achieving your dream. No one else can do it for you. Unless you take the responsibility yourself and decide in your heart that you want to achieve something exceptional, you will be exactly where you are today a year from now. It is your choice and it is your dream. It is your responsibility to achieve your dream.

Dreams Sustain Us

When Mary Kay's husband died, she unexpectedly lost the man who loved, supported, and encouraged her. At the time of his death, she was two weeks from starting up her new company Mary Kay Cosmetics, and was faced with a difficult decision. She had just lost her husband, had only $5,000 to her name and was on the brink of taking a huge risk: Enriching women's lives was her dream. She sat down with her family and sought their advice as to what she should do considering the loss of her husband. Her loss had caused her to question many things in her life, including her decision to start her own business. Her family told her that she needed to pursue her dream. She had worked for others throughout her entire life, and now she had a dream as well as a plan. She decided to go for it.

Lupita Ceballos

In 1996, I was at a point in my business at which I began questioning myself and my abilities. I was not burned out, I just felt stagnant. That year at Mary Kay's annual seminar, I heard Lupita Ceballos speak. Lupita and her husband were from Mexico. Her husband was a successful physician in Mexico, but they both longed to come to America and pursue their dreams.

During her speech, Lupita talked about the challenges of emigrating from Mexico, learning English, and trying to find a way to achieve her dream. At the time of this seminar, Lupita had become a top Sales Director, with twice the sales I had been able to achieve in my career.

After her speech, I knew I had to talk with Lupita about her life and experiences. I needed some direction.

I met her in the hall and spoke with her for a while. I told her about my frustration and asked her for her feedback. Lupita explained that the problem was not my dream, but my action. She went on to explain how she got up very early every morning to plan her day. She explained how she had an action plan for each day that ensured success. Lupita also made sure she had balance in her life: God first, family second, career third. Lupita challenged me to take charge of my dream and follow through with actions that would ensure the outcome I desired.

The following year, I lived the principles that Lupita had taught me. With the Mary Kay opportunity, when you achieve your goals, you are rewarded. In 1997, I received an award for achieving my goal. You can imagine how excited I was to achieve my goals and travel to the Greek Islands as a reward for my accomplishments. One of the others who had qualified for the trip was Lupita. It was fitting that I got to enjoy my reward with the woman who had inspired me to pursue my dreams with action.

An Action Plan for Your Dream

A good idea is only good if you execute it. The same is true for dreams. You may have the most wonderful dreams imaginable, but if you do not choose to execute your dreams, you might as well not have them. A few steps that can help you achieve your dream follow:

- *Define your dream.* If you want to achieve something, you need to be sure that you understand exactly what it is. You must spend time thinking about that dream. You must realize that dreams are a little like movies: Some movies are in black and white; others are in color. You need to define your dream with all the details in full color. It needs to have life. Make small notes or signs and put them everywhere, on your vanity, on your refrigerator, on the steering wheel of your car . . . hey, why not laminate it and put it in your shower. I call it SHOWER POWER.

- *Develop your plan.* The next step is to develop a plan for achieving your dream. You must think in terms of exactly what you have to do every day in order to achieve your dreams. Your plan must focus on the actions you must undertake to reach your goal. You must have a daily plan, along with an overall understanding of how your daily plan fits into your long-term goal. Write down a six-most-important-things-to-do list prior to going to sleep, putting your most difficult task first and then list the others in order of importance.
- *Be accountable.* It is essential that you have a friend or family member who will hold you accountable to your plan. No one needs a nag, but we do need someone who cares for us who will help us make sure we are consistent in carrying out our daily plans. Find a mentor in your life like I found in Lupita and so many other top Sales Directors with whom I am friends.
- *Celebrate milestones.* You might consider forming an accountability group as part of your plan. It is important that you take time to celebrate your accomplish-

ments. An accountability group can help you understand the challenges that others face. Your feelings are no different from anyone else's. It's also great to celebrate your victories with a group of fellow dreamers. A word of caution here: Work with like-minded people who are big dreamers like you. Reach up to those who have gone before you.

- *Balance.* Success is about life and family. It's not about money. It is really important that you make sure you never lose your life's balance: God first, family second, and career third. I use a 30-day erasable calendar each month to help me keep my life in balance and to allow my family to see it. We set goals first of all at the beginning of the month as a family and then we spill those goals into timelines on the calendar. We even color code it. There is then harmony in your house. There is a Chinese proverb that says, "When there is harmony in the household, there is order in the nation."

Go for Your Dreams

Just about everyone has a dream. I can recall lying in bed in Ireland often crying myself to sleep out of the frustration of wanting more in my life. God planted in my heart and soul a dream of coming to the United States and divine intervention kicked in when I opened my mind to the wondrous possibilities that God allows and I took action. I am a huge believer that if God has given you a dream then he has given you the ability to achieve that dream.

At some point, you may have given up on your dream. At another, you may have allowed circumstances to put a hold on your dreams. I want you to take a moment and think about the following questions: What are your dreams? Is there a dream that you have given up on? I challenge you to write down your dreams. By the end of this day, I want you to write up an action plan for achieving your dreams. I suggest that you create a goal poster complete with pictures that provide images of your personal goals. Now, make the conscious decision to work at achieving your dreams. It will change your life! After that tragedy of the USS Cole, the commander was quoted as saying, "Those men and women who died defending our freedom; they had dreams in their heart with their families a part of their dreams. They will never get to live out their dreams. Your responsibility as an American citizen is to live out your dream so you can give their life meaning."

I hope you have taken the time to complete that list of your dreams. I also asked you to supplement that with a plan for achieving your dreams. Finally, I hope you made the commitment to achieve daily goals that relate to those dreams. It basically gets down to three words: dream, plan, and act. Create your dream list, develop a personal plan for success, and then go for it!

Only you can achieve your dreams. Your dreams are what inspire you to go beyond what you think you can do. You must make the commitment today to begin putting action behind your dreams. If you do not, no one else will.

Chapter 12

Avoid Sabotaging Yourself

The subject of self-sabotage and its occurrence in our lives is a complex and challenging issue to address. The reasons it is so difficult to recognize and resolve behaviors that lead to self-sabotage has to do with its basic nature. Self-sabotage is almost always invisible to the one who does it. Individuals who sabotage their own lives are usually unaware that they are responsible for impeding their own happiness. Because we tend to blame other people or external factors for our failures or shortcomings, we rarely scrutinize our choices and behaviors or consider how they shape our lives.

Even if a person acknowledges their lack of action and poor decision-making skills, it is difficult to remedy self-sabotage because it often relates to events in our past, and involves unconscious actions or behaviors we are unwilling to face. The truth is that whether we want it to or not, our childhood experiences stay with us for our entire lives. The lessons learned, even the bad ones, remain with us long after childhood.

For example, the shy individual who is convinced that she is unable to meet new people or make a sales presentation is more often than not, living out a lesson she learned as a child. In most cases, as children, these individuals received messages from their parents that they were not good, or that they could not speak. At some point, those behaviors developed into shyness. It is a lesson that is clearly self-defeating, but often the lessons we learn as children are very powerfully taught. For that reason, they are difficult to correct.

When children are neglected or emotionally abused by their parents, they grow up harboring anger and resentment. Typically, individuals who are overly critical of other people are dealing with a lot of psychological anger. This psychological anger can present itself in various ways and in many cases, is rooted in a desire to control others. People who are angry often become critical of other people in an effort to change them.

One of the surprising ways that anger comes out is through procrastination. Procrastination is a form of controlling behavior. In my experience, I've seen many people fail at the sales business because they procrastinate. They never get around to making appointments.

The person who is always late is also asserting control over others by being consistently late. Such behaviors are clearly self-sabotage and you must do your best to avoid these behaviors. They ruin relationships, prevent you from accomplishing goals, and contribute to failed sales careers.

Overcoming Self-Sabotage

Kim Ogden's life was much like a lot of our lives a few years ago. Kim had worked her way into a wonderful position at a good company and seemed to have things together. She was the sole administrative assistant in an architectural firm. She loved what she did and, at first, thought that she would stay at the firm for the remainder of her career.

Kim seemed very outgoing when it came to strangers. She must have gotten that trait from her father who was one of those people who "never met a stranger." But there was another side of Kim. She had experienced a number of events in her childhood that resulted in extremely high levels of insecurity in her adult life and, as a consequence, she resisted interpersonal intimacy and closeness. The way Kim dealt with her insecurities was to cover up her shyness with her seemingly outgoing personality. In many ways, Kim was torn between these two different aspects of her personality.

While she was working at her full-time job at the architecture firm, Kim became interested in personal fitness. She loved working out. It was something she could do alone and it made her feel good about herself. There was just one problem: Kim was really good at personal fitness. Kim was so gifted at personal fitness that wherever she went, people would ask her questions or seek her help. That created a problem for Kim who was basically a shy person. In spite of her shyness, Kim decided to pursue personal training as a part-time career in addition to her job at the architect firm. She began taking classes and obtaining the certifications to become a fitness instructor. It was not long before Kim had a growing personal training business on the side.

On the outside, Kim was the picture of self-confidence. On the inside, she was dealing with continual feelings of low self-esteem. Despite her insecurities, Kim became interested in starting her own fitness center. She convinced a number of former professional football players to finance her endeavor. She did her homework, found a location, and had even decided on the equipment she would buy. In spite of all of this success, Kim still had feelings of low self-esteem.

Divine Intervention

One day while Kim was working out at the fitness center, a man walked up to her and said, "I've been watching you work with your clients. You would be great at the business my wife is in. Is there any way I could introduce you to her?" Kim asked the man a few questions, and he explained that his wife was an Independent Beauty Consultant. Kim was nice, but firm. She did not use make up because of an allergy and certainly had no interest in hearing about selling cosmetics. Kim was in the final stages of starting her own fitness business, so she really had no interest in what the man was saying. Finally, the man asked if he could give her his wife's card. She took it, but threw it in the trash when she got back to the locker room. Kim continued to work on opening her own fitness center over the next few weeks.

A month later, Kim walked into the gym and saw the man that had approached her about his wife's business; this time, he was exercising with his wife. Kim recalls how she immediately turned and went the other direction in an attempt to escape the man. The persistent man followed her with his wife and introduced her to Kim.

Kim thought that the woman was friendly enough and exchanged the usual pleasantries with her. Then, she proceeded to begin her own workout. The man's wife, Marlys Skillings, decided to follow Kim around and do her workout alongside Kim. They talked a bit between exercises but Kim still had no interest in selling cosmetics. Marlys suggested that they go to lunch together, and Kim agreed.

During lunch, Marlys told Kim about the opportunities at Mary Kay. "It took me all of 15 minutes to realize that this was something that I had to do," said Kim. She realized that in spite of her feelings of insecurity, she did have a knack for walking up to absolute strangers and striking up a conversation, just like her father did. Marlys then invited Kim to go to have a complementary facial so she could see just how well the products worked. Kim explained to Marlys that she had no intention of ever using Mary Kay products due to her skin allergies.

Marlys explained that she did not have to use the product, and Kim was on her way to her new Mary Kay business. Interestingly, Kim did begin using the product and found that it worked very well for her. She's a committed user now and never leaves home without her make up "perfectly applied."

I spoke to Kim about the circumstances that led to her beginning her Mary Kay business. "It was like the Lord intervened in my life. Here I was getting ready to start my own business, I had raised a lot of money, and in 15 minutes my future plans were changed," said Kim. Kim abandoned her plans to start a fitness business because she felt that the Mary Kay opportunity offered her much more potential.

One of the most inspiring transformations I see in successful Mary Kay Consultants is a metamorphosis from feelings of extreme insecurity to confidence and poise when it came to interpersonal relationships and public speaking. In spite of her apparent self-confidence in public, Kim was a person who really struggled with feelings of insecurity. When she first began her Mary Kay business, that did not change. She was still terrified of the idea of speaking in public. Like others who encountered the same difficulty, Kim was able to overcome the problem with the encouragement of her Mary Kay friends.

Kim's first five years as a Beauty Consultant went extremely well. One of the things that Kim had to work on was her feelings of inadequacy and low self-esteem. Like so many others who have joined the Mary Kay family, Kim discovered that it was the women around her who were finally able to convince her that she was a talented woman. Kim often says, "Mary Kay convinced me to get out of my own way." Kim had been allowing her feelings of insecurity to sabotage her business decisions. Once she made the decision that she was going to change, she was well on her way.

In 1995, Kim was on track to grow her business to the point that she could potentially qualify for the position of Independent National Sales Director. She had become close friends with many of her Mary Kay "sisters" and life was absolutely wonderful. It was during this time that Kim was asked to keep her three-year-old niece. Kim did not hesitate, even though it required her to be available to care for the little girl 24 hours a day. Kim made the commitment and cared for the girl for one year.

Kim's ability to care for the niece, because of the flexibility of her business, has made a world of difference in the little girl's life. Kim was able to step in and help her niece at a most critical time in the little girl's life.

After taking a year out of her life to care for her niece, Kim decided to have a child of her own.

Again, being in business for herself and her ability to determine her own schedule, workload, and responsibilities is what made the difference. Kim admits that taking nine years away from her business to care for her sister's child and raising her own child, has temporarily slowed the growth of her business. Now that her daughter is eight years old, Kim is ready to pick up where she left off in her quest for success. Kim told me that she is again on the way to becoming a National Sales Director. I know she can do it, because she figured out how to avoid the self-sabotage that could have sidetracked her for life. Because she was able to understand her own barriers to success and overcome them, she has been able to step in and take control of her life and care for her family.

Recognizing Self-Sabotage

Psychological anger that is rooted in your childhood can sabotage your life as well as your career. I have consistently found that there are three habits that salespeople have that sabotage their sales success:

1. Thinking (and talking) in terms of "me."
2. Focusing on the sale instead of the customer.
3. Manipulating the sale.

These are common practices among some salespeople. Salespeople who use these behaviors have to work significantly harder to achieve what they could with half the effort.

Thinking (and Talking) in Terms of "Me"

During a sales call, salespeople should not talk about their likes or dislikes. Customers are more concerned with whether or not you can fulfill their needs than what your tastes are. One way to spot a poor salesperson is to note how many times she says "I" or "me" during a sales call.

Being an ego-driven person is simply another way of engaging in self-sabotage. People do not want to buy from people who do not have the customer's needs as their priority. The key is to learn to seek the best for others.

Focusing on the Sale instead of the Customer

A friend of mine who was shopping for disability insurance encountered a salesperson who attempted to make a sale by saying; "I don't like to end a sales call without selling something." My friend was tempted to respond, "I don't care what you like or don't like." She made it clear that she did not need his product. My friend simply walked away. My friend said that after the salesperson said that, there was absolutely no way she would ever do business with that salesperson again. Futilely, the salesperson continued to call my friend for a couple of years.

Manipulating the Sale

When a salesperson sends a message to a customer that he thinks she is somewhat stupid, the customer really does figure it out. Manipulation is another way that companies and people lose a customer for life.

Avoid Self-Sabotage

There are numerous ways to engage in self-sabotage. A way to ensure that you do not fall into the self-sabotage trap is to sporadically make joint presentations with another salesperson. It's a good idea to make an arrangement with someone who cares enough for you to tell you the truth. It's also important to work together at least once every six months. As the most seasoned sales professionals will tell you, it's always a good idea to make sure you have not picked up any bad habits along the way. If everything you do is in the best interests of your customer, you probably do not have anything to worry about.

Chapter 13

Perseverance

When I first began my business, I did not have what I would consider a high level of perseverance. I only began to understand the idea of perseverance about five years into my Mary Kay business. Perseverance is the result of not only a positive attitude about life, but a solid vision for your future.

In spite of my early life—being born into a highly regarded family, being shunned after my father's untimely death, and watching my mother end up almost penniless—I did not grow up to be a person with a strong sense of perseverance. That is why I believe perseverance is something that is learned throughout someone's life rather than something that develops in childhood. Some people react to the difficulties of life by adopting an attitude of defeat, but for those who have a dream for their lives, life's setbacks are simply stepping stones on the path toward success. That is where the idea of a vision for your life comes in.

Early in my childhood, I realized that I wanted to be successful enough to be able to repay my mother for all of the sacrifices she made for my brother, my sisters, and me. I knew that was what I wanted to do, but I had no vision of what I wanted to become or how I would achieve my dreams. In a way, my personal vision for my life began when I first saw the Statue of Liberty. Gazing at the statue, I realized that there had been millions of people, just like me, who had come to this wonderful land to fulfill their dreams of freedom, opportunity, and achievement.

In the journey of life, we are faced with many hardships and difficult decisions, but it is up to you to choose to treat these hardships as obstacles or as opportunities in disguise. I learned from my mentor and Senior National Sales Director years ago that no one can upset me, make me angry, or hurt my feelings without my permission. Who have you allowed to take away the control of your life? If you are to persevere, you *must* control how you think. That means you must reaffirm your dream as you deal with each setback in life. It means that you reaffirm that you are a winner and not a loser. It means that you reaffirm your dream and your commitment to persevere in pursuing that dream. The power of affirmation is huge in my life.

What I challenge you to do is to write out an affirmation on your life. An example of an affirmation is, "Every day in every way I get better and better." Or, "God has a huge purpose and plan for my life." Determine your personal goals, repeat your affirmation daily, and notice the difference in your life. Continuously reminding yourself of your purpose and your goals will keep you persevering when events or people in your life try to divert you from an opportunity.

I often use two words when I speak about achieving goals: One is persistence, the other is perseverance. It is crucial to our success to be persistent in achieving our goals. Our perseverance helps keep us focused on our ultimate goal. If we maintain our focus on our goals, we will be inspired to continually work toward those goals. Being persistent means that we live our lives keeping our dreams before us at all times.

Living with Our Life-Goals in Mind

In 2003, the news media was full of a story about a mountain climber who had cut off his own arm to save his life. The man had unwisely ventured into a remote mountain area alone. He fell and a boulder crashed down on him, pinning his arm. He was trapped and there was no way for him to escape . . . but one. He had to cut off his own arm.

The man had but one goal in light of his circumstances. He wanted to live. He tried and tried to free his pinned arm, but the boulder was just too heavy for him to move. Finally, he decided that the only way for him to live was to cut off his own arm. Somehow he managed to do it, and because of that he is alive today. He persevered where others might have given up and died.

Every day you make decisions that will impact the rest of your life. If you allow the apparent impossibility of your circumstances to overcome your will, you will fail. If you decide that you will persevere despite adversity, more often than not you will succeed. You cannot allow the discouragement of the moment to destroy the dream of your life. To become a success in life, you must make perseverance the cornerstone of your mission in life.

One Consultant who has demonstrated persistence in her life is Ava Oja, an Independent Senior Sales Director. Ava grew up in a house that was filled with abuse. Like me, she grew up in a house with an alcoholic parent. From her earliest years, Ava's father and her mother physically abused her. She was often awakened during the night to be beaten. She was constantly told that she was stupid.

One "ritual" that Ava had to endure was dinnertime beatings. Often, without warning, her mother would come over to her and knock her off of her chair onto the floor. Even though the beatings continued until she was 13 years old, Ava was not able to defend herself. By that age, Ava was taller than her mother, but her father told Ava that if she lifted her hand against her mother, he would finish the job for her mother. Ava was required to lie on the floor and endure the beatings.

As if her life was not already difficult enough, Ava endured another traumatic event when she was 12. She was raped. Already intimidated and abused, Ava chose to keep the incident a secret since she knew that it would trigger even more abuse from her parents.

Due to a genetic flaw, she was born with only six teeth. During the beatings, her family would threaten to take away her false teeth. She was terrified by the thought of going to school with no teeth, and having her schoolmates make fun of her. One evening, after Ava had endured an unusually severe beating, she decided to call the police. Two officers came and removed her from the home. Ava thought that at last she would be able to live in a home where there was no violence. Instead, the judge ordered that she be sent to a juvenile facility for six months. Threatened and intimidated by other juveniles on a daily basis, Ava was terrified to be there.

When she was finally placed in her first foster home, she was one of 10 children in the home. She was fed only meager meals of Spam or an occasional bowl of rice for supper. After a few months, she was placed in another home, but there was sexual abuse taking place in that home. Finally, she was placed in another home, but the conditions were not much better than the previous two.

Ava decided at age 15 to strike out on her own. Over the years, Ava had held one part-time job after another. At the age of 17, she became pregnant, and just six months before her eighteenth birthday, gave birth to a baby girl. Although it broke her heart, she gave the child up for adoption since she could not care for her.

Once she turned 18 and the court declared her an independent, she moved to Alaska where she became a bartender. She also met her husband in Alaska and had her son. That marriage lasted only a short time due to abuse.

Ava continued her life as a single mom. When her son Michael was 11 years old, Ava had an accident that would change the rest of her life. In January of 1988, Ava was at work one day and had to climb a ladder in the store where she worked. She accidentally fell to the concrete floor. Her back was broken in numerous places and she was paralyzed from the waist down. Ava was told that she would never walk again.

At that time, Ava was in her early 30s, a single mom, and unable to work. Ava, in spite of all of her difficulties, had become a woman of perseverance. She was unwilling to give in to her injury, and insisted that she would again learn to walk. By May 1988, she was walking again.

Ava loved to dance and one of the promises she made to herself was that she would dance again. Ava did get to dance again, but in 1989 there were more changes in Ava's life. She met her husband Warren. They were married in 1990. Warren became the father that her son Michael had never had. Warren loved him and cared for him just as if Michael were his own son.

In 1996, Ava was involved in another accident. An uninsured driver hit her car from behind. Ava suffered a number of injuries to her neck, but worse than that, the accident triggered the onset of fibromyalgia, causing her constant pain. In 1998, Ava started her Mary Kay business. At that time, her business began to take off. Ava qualified for the use of a Mary Kay career car, and everything seemed to be going well. Undeterred by yet another setback and the problems from the fibromyalgia, Ava went on to achieve her other goals for her Mary Kay business.

No amount of success could prepare Ava for what she faced in 1999. Late one evening, she and Warren got a call that her son Michael had been killed in a motorcycle accident.

Heartbreak often does more than simply cause grief. It can also lead to depression and impact a person's physical health as well. Ava endured all of those as she tried to cope with the loss of her son. Ava told me about what a wonderful, respectful young man he had become. Ava, Michael, and Warren had become a family. One of the letters Ava got after her son died was from an Alaska state senator who had known of Michael. In that letter, the Senator spoke of what a fine young man Michael had been.

Some people who grow up in difficult circumstances simply give up. Others develop a high degree of perseverance. Ava is a person who lives perseverance. Just as she had overcome each of the tragedies of her life, she struggled to persevere despite the loss of her son. Ava wrote me a note expressing her thoughts and feelings about what she has endured. She began with a few thoughts about her beloved Michael:

> He grew up knowing that God doesn't make losers, he makes WINNERS! That if you wanted to succeed at anything you must not quit on yourself. Disappointments are just learning opportunities; you revamp and continue on. My son Michael touched a lot of lives in his short life and also made a difference in many of those lives. He had a WINNER'S Attitude. One day he told me that his attitude came from me being a part of the Mary Kay world. He was recognized for his great attitude on many occasions at his job. My husband Warren (his dad) and I were very proud of the man he had grown into.
>
> I am so very appreciative to God for allowing me to have Michael for as long as I did. He is loved and missed every moment of each day. I am also proud of myself for stepping out of my own box and building a business with Mary Kay that allowed my son to benefit. That would not have happened if I hadn't felt the fear and DID it anyway!

Ava's life is one that is almost unimaginable to most of us. Mary Kay Ash, the founder of Mary Kay Inc., was divorced by her first husband after he returned from World War II. She was left alone to raise three young children, and she had no job. Mary Kay overcame her obstacles and went on to have a successful sales career in direct marketing. During her work life prior to forming Mary Kay Inc. she was able to achieve success by working her way up to senior management positions at a couple of major direct marketing companies.

After a successful 25-year career Mary Kay had worked her way up to the senior sales position at one company. Mary Kay Ash was asked to train a young man. After he completed his training, she learned that he was in line to receive a significant promotion and become her boss. That is when Mary Kay decided to retire and write a book. Not long after that, she was inspired to come out of retirement and create a company that was dedicated to helping women.

It takes perseverance to succeed. Most people with Ava's background do not go on to have successful careers. Most women of Mary Kay's generation resigned themselves to their diminished role in the male-dominated corporate world. Ava Oja and Mary Kay Ash demonstrated that any differences we make in our lives are a result of perseverance.

I believe in miracles, and perseverance allows women to achieve miracles. I want to share a saying with you that may inspire you to become a person of perseverance:

> Don't quit . . . five minutes before the miracle happens!

You can live the miracles of your life if you decide to become an individual who lives the principle of perseverance. In the game of life, quitting is not an acceptable option. Perseverance is what allows you to achieve your potential. Perseverance is the road you travel between your dream and your success. No one promised you it was going to be easy, but I promise you that if you are willing to persevere, you will achieve your life's dreams. You can live a miracle.

Perseverance, Practically Speaking

Before there were tractors to till the soil, farmers used to walk behind a horse and a plow to till a field. In some parts of the world, they still plow in that manner.

When a farmer starts off to plow a field, he does not look down at the ground. He picks out a point on the other end of the field and keeps his eyes on that point. It might be a tree or a fence post, but the farmer understands that if he takes his eyes off of his target, he will be unable to plow a straight line. That is how perseverance works as well.

When it comes to achieving your life dreams, you are just like that farmer. In order to persevere, you have to pick out your dream and never take your eyes off of it. If you do not do this, you will be a lot like a farmer who fails to pick out a target when plowing: Your path will be crooked and if you do finally get to your goal, it will be little more than an accident. Perseverance is all about adding a life commitment to your life dreams. You absolutely must keep your eyes focused on your life dreams if you are to persevere.

Chapter 14

No Excuses

There is a saying that "Winners have goals, losers make excuses." Excuses are attempts to explain why you have given up. Worse than that, excuses are attempts to shift the blame from you to something or someone else.

In our relationship with God, family, and work, we must learn to take responsibility for what we do. We cannot lie to God, and if we try to lie it damages our fellowship with Him. We cannot lie to family. We cannot make excuses about why we are not fulfilling our role as a mother, father, or child to the best of our ability. Ultimately, we cannot make excuses about work. If we want to be successful in life, we have to take responsibility for our own lives and our own success.

Making excuses is little different from lying: At some point, it becomes difficult to figure out which stories you have told and which ones you have not. It is much easier to live each day based on the truth. This applies to every aspect of our lives.

When it comes to our relationship with God, we cannot make excuses for ourselves, because we are aware of the truth in our minds and in our hearts and that is where God dwells. In a family situation, when people live their lives in denial of why they have failed to perform appropriately, their lives become a *pattern of excuses.* It's that pattern of excuses that is detrimental to our relationships. If I put my business above the needs of Vince and Vince Jr. and make excuses for it, they will immediately notice. If I am making excuses, it means that I am aware of what I should have done in the first place, and I know that I am wrong. At some point, if I am neglecting my duties as a wife and mother, their relationship and behavior toward me will change as well. That is a lose-lose situation no matter who you are. There is a reason that God first, family second, and work third results in a balanced life. It simply means that we are putting our priorities in the right order.

Another consequence of relying on a pattern of excuses is that, at some point, the pattern influences how you think and who you are. In other words, you begin to live your life as if what you have said is really true. Ultimately, you lose your focus on reality and your job as a mother or wife. Worse yet, you have begun to destroy the quality of the relationships between you and your family and your ability to succeed at work. If you care for someone or something, you do not lie to them, and excuses are lies constructed to justify actions.

A pattern of excuses will create failure in a sales career. The most important behavior you can adopt as a salesperson is to tell yourself and others the truth. Only then, will you be able to achieve success. Further, when you learn to turn a pattern of excuses into telling the truth, others will be able to help you get on the right track. Why waste your time telling yourself lies?

Right On!

Martha Reedy is a Sales Consultant who has chosen to avoid living a life characterized by a pattern of excuses. After all, what would you expect from a schoolteacher? I am sure she's heard "My dog ate my homework" more than once in her life. Martha is the kind of person people love to be around. She is straight forward, enthusiastic, and "right on."

Martha has been working in her own business for about four years. She continues to pursue a career that is her passion: Teaching disabled children. Her entry into the Mary Kay business was a bit of a fluke. About five years ago, Martha had agreed to visit with a friend who was selling Mary Kay products. On the day of her appointment, Martha had a list of things she needed to do, so when her friend proposed she think about selling Mary Kay products, she quickly replied "yes." Her friend was a little shocked, because she had barely begun to tell

Martha about the opportunity. But Martha had decided that the best way to get rid of the friend and get on with her day was to agree to the proposition so she could move on to those really important things she needed to do.

It took Martha a few months to get started, but when she finally got around to kicking off her business, she became excited about the prospect. It was not long before Martha's business took off. One day, Martha's husband asked her how the business was going. Martha had allowed a lot of inventory to build up around the house, and her husband was concerned. He politely asked that Martha sell her inventory so that they could clean out their house.

Martha decided he was right and she hit the sales trail with the purpose of decreasing her inventory. Again she was successful. That is when she decided she would try to earn the use of a career car. Not long after making the commitment, Martha earned the use of her career car. Once she had the car, Martha decided to set a goal of achieving Sales Director status. After a four-month qualifying period, Martha again hit her goal and became a Sales Director.

Rather than offering excuses about why she cannot do something, Martha consistently sets goals for herself and goes for them. Martha continues to gain recognition for her sales accomplishments. She has been recognized at the annual Mary Kay Seminar for her stellar performance on a number of occasions.

You might ask why someone with a successful career might choose to pursue another one. I think the answer is in a note that I recently got from Martha:

> Mary Kay has enriched my life because I have a close friend, Gillian Ortega, and because being a Consultant I can brighten and enrich so many lives by bringing hope and pampering beauty into their daily routine. But most of all because I can fulfill a promise made to myself for my mom. . . . making the people that are inflicted with myasthenia gravis [a muscle and nerve degenerating disease that can be fatal] a little bit happier. For the past four years, I have been teaching skin care and giving products to the people that have been inflicted with this disease in the Kansas/Missouri area. To them I'm known as the Mary Kay angel; Thank you, Mary Kay Inc., for giving me the opportunity to fulfill my dreams.
>
> As for my school teaching, like I said before: Why not have the best of both worlds: enlightening children during the day and enriching moms at night. Who could ask for anything more? Both are priceless!!! Why drop one for the other?

Martha is truly a "no excuses" person. She inspires me with her tenacity and her attitude. If you have not figured it out by now, most of the people I meet do not sell Mary Kay products for the money. They are on a mission to help others, and their sales business is how they do it. After all, that is what sales is all about: Seek the best for others.

Becoming a "No Excuses" Person

Psychologists will tell you that their job is to try to get people to be honest with themselves. Associating with people who often give themselves excuses can be taxing. You must be careful dealing with people like that. Being blunt or straightforward with people who are dealing with extreme personal issues, can create more problems than it solves. That is why in psychotherapy it can take a long time for someone to gain a realization of why they exhibit certain behaviors.

If you have people in your life who rely on excuses and self-defeating behaviors, you must leave the psychologist role to a trained professional. The only person you can change is yourself. Everyone has areas of their lives in which they are untrue to themselves. To recognize and change the patterns of making excuses, you must be introspective. If you are a person who practices a pattern of making excuses, you are the only one who can change that. Becoming a "no excuses" person can be an easy process.

The first step is to place a wide rubber band around your wrist. Write the words "stay strong" on it. Spend one day focusing in and evaluating everything you say. When you hear yourself offering an excuse, snap the rubber band to remind yourself of your new commitment. That is one way of recognizing whether you have a personal pattern of excuses. As many times as you snap the rubber band is as many times as you made excuses.

The second step involves taking notes regarding your excuses. Each time you snap the rubber band, write yourself a note about the excuse that you gave. At the end of the day, sit down and review the list. Were your excuses just ways of avoiding personal accountability? Were the situations you made excuses about really unavoidable? Were there other options or actions you could have taken to accomplish something instead of giving an excuse? You will find that most, if not all, of your excuses were simply that: A means to avoiding personal accountability.

The human mind is a phenomenal thing. If you are willing to spend two days focusing on your words and behaviors, you will find that they will begin to change. This exercise brings consciousness to thoughts and behaviors you might be unconscious of and will help you change them. You might be sitting at lunch having a conversation when you find yourself snapping that rubber band. At some point, you will probably smile because you recognize what you are doing. Explaining your process to your lunch mate will also empower them. Imagine how you might change more lives than just your own.

This process helps you focus on a counterproductive habit in a relatively painless way. When you are able to think in more rational terms, you will begin to act in more rational terms. Excuses are not rational. When you remove excuses from your thinking, you remove them from your behavior, which inevitably produces positive results.

Another exercise that can help break the cycle of excuses requires asking for the help of a trusted friend whom you are confident wants the best for you. A person who is normally very critical and disparaging is not suited for this task. The first step is to ask your friend to observe your behaviors and interactions and commit to hold you accountable for yourself. If she agrees, she has two responsibilities: First, point out times that you rely on using excuses. Second, ask the individual if he or she is willing to set up a time to meet with you on a periodic basis, preferably weekly.

These weekly visits will involve discussions about your failures as well as your successes. I recommend asking a friend who has been especially encouraging to you in the past. The purpose of these visits is not to tear you down, but to help you become a "no excuses" person. If you find that you have asked the wrong person, immediately terminate that mentoring relationship.

The Power to Succeed

Becoming a "no excuses" person is not an automatic change. It takes time. You must be prepared to take baby steps. It is often helpful to keep a journal in which you record your victories. This approach helps you to take baby steps. Each time you snap the rubber band, it helps you to recognize and address the issues that are at the root of your behavior in relationships.

Another thing we all have to remember is that excuses are baggage that we bring with us from our past.

Emotional baggage never completely disappears. It can influence our thoughts and behaviors at the most inopportune times. This is something that you must continually be conscious of. All it takes is one rude customer or one small failure and we are back on the wrong track again, thinking like we used to think. That is why "no excuses" is a proactive responsibility. We must be constantly vigilant if we are to overcome the problem.

Sales Resistance

I want to close out this chapter by talking about sales resistance. Sales resistance is a problem that we often encounter with more experienced salespeople. At some point in their careers, experienced salespeople reach a point in which they will do almost anything to avoid making new business calls. That is what causes sales careers to plummet. In most cases, "excuses" are what characterize people who have become sales resistant. Here are some of the "excuses" you might hear from such people:

- I've met my goals and don't need to sell anymore.
- I have too much work to do with existing customers.
- I can handle my customers by phone and e-mail now, I don't need to get out and see people.
- I am really busy; the phone just won't let me go these days.

I have experienced times in my business in which I have used one or more of those excuses. Most of the time, it is a momentary situation. I just need to give myself a little break. I do that by laying low and allowing my sales activities to decrease for a few days. The problem with sales resistance is that it can quickly become a habit. You must remind yourself that a sales professional who is not out working on new business is a sales professional who is on her way down the ladder of performance. When you stop selling new business, you have actually stopped selling. There is no way your business can survive on a long-term basis without new customers.

This caveat especially refers to experienced salespeople. That is the reason so many sales organizations continually train and retrain their people. We all need an occasional kick in the pants in order to make sure we do not allow our enthusiasm to cool off.

Make No Excuses

I encourage you to think seriously about how excuses impact your life. Many great people would have never have made it if they had allowed excuses to rule their lives. You have a reason to be successful. It doesn't matter whether you are a teacher, a housewife, or a sales professional, you have a reason to be successful. You have the ability to succeed. You must accept the challenge that God gave you to maximize the person He made you. With that in mind, I would like to leave you with the following statement:

> Excuses are lies that keep us from achieving our potential and inactivity is the darkroom where negatives are developed.

PART IV

Closing Comments

Chapter 15

God, Family, and Work

If there have been blessings in my life, they have been in the order of God, family, and work. Mary Kay lived that principle. That is why she was not only successful, but happy as well.

I cannot remember a time in my life in which God was not important. I remember my years as a young girl in Ireland when my family was struggling and how God often carried me through those difficult times. I understood early on the importance of family. My mother, brother, and sisters were able to survive because we were a family. My mother pulled us together with her love. In many ways, we were much more fortunate than other families around us, they had money and we had none, but we had a powerful family life filled with love.

As I think about my family life today, those are the priorities that allow me to have peace, security, and my work. My God has never failed me, even in those darkest days. My family, and that includes Vince's family, loves me unconditionally. And finally, I have a business that inspires me to wake up in the morning and look forward to the day ahead. That is exactly what most people want. The sad reality is, a lot of people do not have that, and it is right there for them to have.

It's Not "All about Me"

I do not know where it came from, but recently I have heard a saying, "It's all about you." I have heard that phrase used in a humorous manner, but in reality it is not a positive affirmation. It is a saying, which if true, tells you that you should live your life around your own needs instead of being concerned about the needs of others.

When our lives achieve the priorities of God first, family second, work third, we are then ready to live our lives as God intended. In the book of Job, when Job lost everything, he lost family then wealth. When Job's life was restored, he restored his relationship with God, then his family, and finally his work. Job makes it clear that the key to his life was his close relationship with God.

Life is not "all about me." Life is all about God, my family, and finally me and my business. This is a philosophy that clearly has biblical origins and that is why it works for those who set those priorities in their lives. We have all seen people who have become consumed with and by their careers. In many cases, those people end up sacrificing marriage and family relationships. Balance is the key to happiness in life.

God First

Denying God and His presence in our lives is little more than arrogance. We did not create ourselves, God did. Our wonderful world has order and all things operate within a design that could not be an accident. It is God's creation. You are God's creation.

"You shall love the Lord your God with all your heart, and with all your soul, and all your might." God also said, "You shall love your neighbor as yourself."[1] Jesus was explaining that "God first" should be the foundation of our lives. Loving God is how we should live our lives. Jesus also said that we are to love our neighbors as ourselves.

Arrogance is not a good quality for a sales relationship, or for any relationship for that matter. Humility, rather than arrogance, will draw people to you, help you gain their trust, and enable you to live your life honestly. If we want to achieve the potential that God has given us, we need to be willing to be humble before God. We need to live lives in which we love God with all our heart, soul, and mind. It is really not a question of whether or not

[1] Matthew 22:37; Matthew 22:39, *New American Standard Version.*

God created you and me. The question is are we going to love Him in return.

Family Second

Throughout this book, I have referenced the thousands of women who have taken advantage of the Mary Kay opportunity so that they can spend time with their children. That is also the reason I pursued my own Mary Kay business. I have been blessed to be present at just about every major event in my husband's and my son's lives throughout my career. I know many women who cannot make that statement, and I know that they regret not having been able to be there at those special times.

You do not get out of bed in the morning so you can have more things when you die. You get out of bed in the morning so you can have a full life with your family. That is what is important.

Work Third

There is truth to the old adage, "No man on his death bed ever said, 'I wish I had spent more time at the office.'" The key to happiness is balance, and your family is much more important than your work.

Setting Work as your third priority does not mean that you do not achieve excellence in your life. It simply means that you plan your time around God first, family second, and work third. You will be more capable of success in your business if you have the appropriate priorities in your life. That's what the word *balance* is all about. When we have balance in our lives, we tend to be much happier. Diminish your relationship with God or family, and you are unable to be a truly happy person, and this, in turn, will reflect in your business.

Many people, especially stay-at-home moms, ask me how I am able to maintain this balance. The most successful people in the world plan their work around their time with God and family. This may mean that you get up an hour earlier to organize your business for the day. Or it may mean that you continue your workday after you put your children to bed at night. As for me, I am thankful for every day that I have with my family. I am also thankful for a business that allows me to spend those precious moments with my family.

The Rest of the Story

In a previous chapter, I told the story of Ava Oja. I told about how Ava had been raised in an abusive home, battered, raped, and even suffered an injury that threatened to cripple her for life. I also told you about how Ava had a daughter as a teenager and gave her up for adoption, and how her life turned around when she met her husband Warren. I also told you about the tragic loss of her son Michael. Here is the rest of the story that I did not tell you.

Throughout her life, Ava had never been around religious people. All she had known was abuse. In 1988, God led Ava to Warren, the man who would become the love of her life and the loving father for her son,

Michael. In 1995, an amazing thing happened to Ava. One of her dear Mary Kay friends sat down with her and told her about the love of Jesus Christ. That day, Ava became a Christian.

God has a plan for us, even if we are not aware of it. Ava could not wait to tell her son Michael about what she had discovered. Michael, who had never been exposed to religion before, made the decision to become a Christian as well. I would like to share a scripture with you:

> These things I have written to you who believe in the name of the Son of God in order that you might know that you have eternal life.
>
> 1 John 5:13[2]

If you look back at Ava's note in Chapter 13, you will see the evidence of her faith, and the confidence that Ava has that someday she will again see her beloved Michael.

God first, family second, work third—that is how Ava lives her life. One other scripture passage is a testament to Ava's faith:

> Who shall separate us from the love of Christ? Shall tribulation, or distress, or persecution, or famine, or nakedness, or peril, or sword?
>
> But in all these things we overwhelmingly conquer through Him who loved us. For I am convinced that neither death, nor life, nor angels, nor principalities, nor things present, nor things to come, nor powers, nor

[2] 1 John 5:13, *New American Standard Version.*

> height, nor depth, nor any other created thing, shall be able to separate us from the love of God, which is in Christ Jesus our Lord.[3]

I suspect that you can hear the confidence of God's love in Ava's words in Chapter 13. In many ways, these verses tell the story of Ava's life. Battered, abused, alone, and penniless at times, Ava is an inspiration to us all. She is an example of someone who persevered through the worst of circumstances.

Just a couple of years ago, Ava received a call from a young woman named Gabriele. Gabriele is the daughter that Ava gave up for adoption. Since that time, Ava has established a relationship with Gabriele.

Ava has been very successful in her Mary Kay business. Armed with only a ninth grade education, Ava has become a sales success. She has earned the use of career cars for over twelve years.

But Ava is most excited about the wonderful balance that she now has in her life. As you listen to Ava, it is clear that she is pleased with her achievements, but more than that, her life now has balance: God first, family second, work third.

Go for It!

Although I cannot know what each person's dream is, I can encourage you to do one thing: Go for it! Life is there for you to live. God wants the best for you, but you have a

[3] Romans 8:35; 37–39, *New American Standard Version.*

responsibility to fulfill it. You have to go for it. The individuals whose stories I shared are exactly like you. They all had times in their lives in which they were discouraged. They all felt that they lacked what it took to make it. You can put me on that list as well.

A wise friend once said: "God is not concerned about your *ability* . . . He's concerned about your *availability.*" Success is not measured in dollars, it is measured in the lives you touch and the blessings you receive. We all want to be happy, but we are not all willing to make the commitment to achieve happiness in our lives. Are you available?

I end this book with a simple challenge. Ask yourself if you are willing to make some choices and commitments in your life. Once you have answered them, write them down so that they are visible to you throughout your day.

- Are you willing to reorganize your priorities as follows: God first, family second, and work third?
- Are you willing to achieve dreams? If so, write them down now.
- Are you willing to develop a written plan of achieving your dreams? If so, write that plan right now.
- Are you willing to go for it? Are you willing to make the commitment to be the author of your own success and happiness?
- Are you willing to persevere? Are you willing to get back up if you're knocked down? Are you willing to keep going after you are rejected? Are you willing to look at failure as a stepping stone on the road to success?

I hope you made the commitment to go for it. If you did, pick out a friend who cares for you. Tell them what you have decided and ask them to remind you of your commitments. More than that, find some winners and start associating with them. Winners love to help others become winners. Real winners live the Golden Rule. Find some people who want to help you win and listen to them.

Thankful

God has blessed me with so much. In the dark days of my life, I was lifted up by His encouragement. My mother and my sisters have always been there to help me and inspire me. God led me to my wonderful husband Vince. God has blessed me with a son, Vince Jr.

I am thankful for my business, but it does not end there. What I am most thankful for in my business is the people with whom I have been associated. I have been challenged, loved, and inspired since the moment I discovered Mary Kay. All of the people I have featured in this book have also been an inspiration to me.

I am thankful. I have been given the opportunity to live the American dream. May God bless America, and thank you God, for your love for my family, my business, and me.

Index